THE HIDDEN POWER OF

Prayer
and
Fasting

The Hidden Power of

Prayer
and
Fasting

by
MAHESH CHAVDA

Destiny Image₀ Publishers, Inc.
P.O. Box 310
Shippensburg, PA 17257-0310

"Tapping the Power of the Age to Come."

ISBN 10: 0-7684-2410-0
ISBN 13: 978-0-7684-2410-2

Previously published as ISBN 0-7684-2017-2

For Worldwide Distribution
Printed in the U.S.A.

2 3 4 5 6 7 8 9 10 / 11 10 09 08 07

This book and all other Destiny Image, Revival Press, MercyPlace, Fresh Bread, Destiny Image Fiction, and Treasure House books are available at Christian bookstores and distributors worldwide.

For a U.S. bookstore nearest you, call **1-800-722-6774**.
For more information on foreign distributors, call **717-532-3040**.
Or reach us on the Internet: **www.destinyimage.com**

Endorsements

Mahesh Chavda has experienced God's grace to fast in a way that has borne much fruit. He is a man of deep passion for Jesus, and this love has been his motivation to pursue the deep places in God's heart. Mahesh has profound personal experience in this area. His understanding will be an inspiration and instruction to many. I recommend this book.

—Mike Bickle, Senior Pastor
Metro Christian Fellowship

Few men in our day have fasted and prayed as often and seen the results that Mahesh Chavda has had in his dynamic ministry. This book will invite you into new depths with God.

—John Arnott, Senior Pastor
Toronto Airport Christian Fellowship

It has been one of my great privileges to know and walk with Mahesh Chavda for more than 20 years. His ministry and teachings come from the trenches of experience. This book is more than just another good manual on the "theology of prayer and fasting"—you have in your hands a stick of dynamite loaded with spiritual power and impartation that comes from one of the modern-day pioneers who has walked what he talks. Your hunger for God will grow and your appetite for this world will diminish when you devour this book. Fasting will become a delight and not just a sacrifice!

—Jim W. Goll, Founder
Ministry to the Nations

Contents

＋══════════════＋

What Is the Answer for Stevie?

Early in my walk with Christ, I went to work at a hospital for mentally handicapped children in Lubbock, Texas. Just like Jesus was driven or impelled by the Holy Spirit to go to the wilderness, I was impelled to enter my own wilderness in Texas—and it was this state school for profoundly handicapped children. It was one of the most tragic places I could have chosen. My days there were filled with heartbreaking hours of interaction with broken and hurting children in an atmosphere filled with some of the most foul smells you can imagine. The children I worked with didn't have control over their bowel functions. Many times they would smear excrement all over themselves, over the doors, and over you. I often asked, "Lord, is this You? Did You really guide me here?"

Before long I came to understand that the Lord had brought me there by sovereign appointment to teach me about Himself. That place in Lubbock, Texas, was my own personal school of the

Holy Spirit. In fact, most of the key principles I use in my ministry today I learned in that place.

There were hundreds of little children there, and most of them had basically been "thrown away" or discarded by their parents. Although they were officially "wards of the state," in reality they were little pieces of broken humanity whom nobody wanted and nobody claimed. The Lord said to me, "My Word says if your father and mother forsake you, I will take you up. I want you to go and love these little ones and be My ambassador of love."[1] So I went.

For the first nine hours, I would work with the ambulatory children, those who could walk. Then I would go to the non-ambulatory wards to work with little brain-damaged babies. Many had been born to mothers on heroin, and others landed there after their alcoholic parents had brutally attacked and injured them in fits of rage or alcohol-induced delirium. These babies would stay in the little cribs until they were too big to fit in them, and I would just hold them in my arms and gently rock them in a rocking chair while I prayed in tongues (my prayer language of the Spirit). I just knew Jesus loved them, and I knew that I loved them too. It was as if Jesus broke off a little piece of His heart and put it in me. I truly loved those little children.

THE LORD STARTED HEALING THEM

Suddenly I found that these little ones who were never supposed to walk were walking. One little girl whose official medical file stated that she had been born blind, started seeing and responding! Every time I came into the room, even though I made no noise, she would turn around and look at me while putting her hands out! It's true—the Lord started healing these children.

It was during that time that I was assigned to what was called a "psychology task force" to administer behavior modification techniques to some of the children. These techniques were designed to teach selected 15-, 16-, and 20-year-old children how to tie their shoelaces or go to the bathroom unassisted.

I'll never forget the day I met a 16-year-old boy in that group of children whom I'll call "Stevie."[2] Stevie was a victim of Down syndrome, a moderate to severe form of mental retardation often characterized by reduced mental capacity and certain physical deformities. Stevie was afflicted with something even worse. He was a self-mutilator who was driven to cry out and beat himself in the face constantly.

The staff psychologist at the school had secured permission from state officials in Austin, Texas, to administer electric shock therapy to Stevie for a six-month period. This "negative operant conditioning," as they called it, was meant to modify Stevie's behavior by administering electric shocks any time he beat himself. They graphed his behavior over that period of time, and I saw the graph. He just got worse and worse instead of better. By the time I was there, his face felt like dry alligator skin because he beat himself continuously.

Finally, the attendants tied Stevie's hands in splints so that he couldn't bend his arms to reach his face. The only problem was that the other children in his dormitory ward developed a new game once they figured out that Stevie's hands were bound at his sides. They liked to run up behind him and push him so hard that he would lose his balance and fall down. Since Stevie could no longer instinctively shield his face with his arms because of the splints, every time the kids on the ward played their game and pushed him, Stevie would land facedown on the floor without any way to protect himself or soften the landing.

AN ANSWER FOR STEVIE?

Most of the time we would find him with blood streaming from his nose, lips, and mouth. Whenever I would come, Stevie could sense God's love coming from me and he would put his head on my shoulder and just weep.

Finally I said, *"Lord, You told me that You sent me here to love these children. What is the answer for Stevie?"*

Very clearly I heard the voice of the Holy Spirit say, "This kind goes not out but by prayer and fasting." Although this may be a very familiar Scripture to you, it sounded totally foreign to me. I had attended a Bible university for four years and had earned my bachelor's degree there, but I didn't even know that the Spirit was quoting a Scripture passage to me from Matthew 17:21!

Another thing I'd failed to learn about during my four years of Bible school training was the subject of fasting. I said, *"Fasting—doesn't that mean no food and no water?"* So I didn't eat or drink anything. I didn't realize that when I fasted from food that I would have dreams about fried chicken, baked potatoes, and steaks. I was also unaware of the fact that when you do without water, your priorities will change. By the third day of my fast without water, I began to get jealous every time I heard someone washing his hands in a bathroom sink! One time a person came out of the bathroom and I said, "You know what? You could have been *drinking* that water!" He said, "What?" and I hurriedly said, "No, forget it."

NOW PRAY FOR STEVIE

On the fourth day the Lord spoke to me and said, "You can drink," and so I started drinking water. But I did not break the fast until the fourteenth day and the Lord said, "Now pray for Stevie."

When I arrived for my shift at the school that day, I took Stevie into my little office cubicle and said, "Stevie, I know your mind may not understand what I'm saying, but your spirit is eternal. I want to tell you that I am a servant of the Lord Jesus Christ. I've come to preach good news to you. I want you to know that Jesus Christ came to set the captives free."

Then I said, "In the name of Jesus, you evil spirit of mutilation, you let him go now in the name of Jesus." Suddenly Stevie's body was flung about eight feet away from me and hit the other wall of the cubicle! When Stevie hit the wall, his body was elevated about three feet above the floor, and then he slid down to the floor and let out a long sigh. Immediately I smelled an incredibly foul smell of rotten eggs and burning sulfur in the room, which gradually faded away.

I quickly went to Stevie, cradled him in my arms, and removed his splints while he watched with wide eyes. Then Stevie began to bend his arms and gently feel his face. I watched him softly touch his eyes, his nose, and his ears; then he started sobbing. He had realized that for the first time he was not being driven to beat himself. He was gently touching his face, and he had been delivered! In that unforgettable moment, the Lord revealed to me what a powerful weapon He has given to us to pull down strongholds and set the captives free. Within a few months, all the scabs had fallen off of Stevie's face. He had begun to heal because he had stopped beating himself.

Frankly, you are reading this book because of Stevie, and I thank God for this young man and for the way the Lord used my compassion for his desperate situation to impart to me the divine truth that I am about to impart to you.

SEARCHER FOR THE TRUTH

The miracle that brings you and me together in the pages of this book really began even earlier, in my sixteenth year, in Kenya, East Africa, in 1962. I was raised in a devout Hindu home, and my destiny was already set according to time-honored East Indian tradition: As the son of a Hindu from a high military caste, I was being trained to become a leader in the Hindu community, and I was well-versed in the sacred Hindu writings.

Since one of the chief principles I had been taught from infancy was, "You are a searcher for the truth," I obediently searched for the truth. My parents were from India, though I was born and raised in Kenya. I had won a number of awards, and even though my father died when I was five years old, I was still a member of a privileged class and a high warrior caste in the Hindu world.

My diligent search for the truth took a sudden turn in a new direction on a hot day in 1962 when a Baptist missionary's wife came to our neighborhood to work with some little children. For reasons known only to God, this petite woman from West Texas was led to knock on the front door of a particular home where a devout Hindu family was living to ask for a cup of cold water. I happened to be there, and I happened to be the one who answered the door, so I gave her a cup of water and she gave me a Bible. (Little did either one of us know at the time that our simple exchange of water for the Word would result in the conversion of more than one million people to Jesus Christ in the years to come. Sometimes even our most insignificant works of obedience are destined for far greater purposes than we can imagine!)

I started reading the Bible because, of course, I was searching for truth. That was how I came across the strangest figure I'd ever read about. His name was Jesus Christ. As a searcher for the truth, I was captivated by this holy man's incredible statement: *"And you shall know the truth, and the truth shall make you free."*[3] I said, "Yes, that's right," and read further in the Book of John.

When I read the passage where Jesus said, *"I am the way, the truth, and the life. No one comes to the Father except through Me"* in John 14:6, the blinding scales fell from the eyes of this committed Hindu of the warrior caste who was so proud of his traditions. I was searching for the truth, and suddenly I saw that Jesus Christ was and is *the Truth.* Yet even then I didn't receive Him as Lord and Savior immediately.

THE PRICE WAS TOO GREAT

Despite what I had read in the Bible, I was debating over whether I should become a Christian because the price seemed to be too great to pay. If I dared to confess Christ, I knew I would be rejected by my family, including my mother, and my brothers and sisters; and I would lose any status I had in the Hindu world. In fact, to my knowledge, I would be the *first* in my caste ever to turn his back on the Hindu faith. Finally, I said, "I'm not going to read the Bible anymore. I'm not even going to think about Jesus anymore."

Suddenly I went to sleep. I wasn't knocked on the head, nor did I drift off to sleep. This was something out of the ordinary. All of a sudden my head dropped down on the table and I was instantly taken to a place where I'd never been before. I was walking on streets of gold and I heard the most beautiful voices rising up in harmonies, singing songs I'd never heard before. I saw colors I'd never seen before. I was in perfect ecstasy (which means a lot to a Hindu!).

There was perfection all around me, but suddenly it all faded into insignificance when I saw the Source of perfection walking toward me. I saw a light brighter than 10,000 suns put together, yet it did not hurt my eyes. He came toward me, and somehow I knew that He was the person of Jesus. I'll never forget His eyes. When I looked into their depths, it was as if He had felt every pain in the world and had shed every tear that had ever been shed on earth. Pure love shone from His eyes in perfect combination with victory and triumph. Then He came and put His hands on my shoulders and said, "My little brother...."

Suddenly I woke up and discovered that the Bible I'd received from the little Baptist lady lay open to the Gospel of Matthew, where Jesus spoke to the rich young ruler:

Jesus said to him, "If you want to be perfect, go, sell what you have and give to the poor, and you will have treasure in heaven; and come, follow Me."

But when the young man heard that saying, he went away sorrowful, for he had great possessions. Then Jesus said to His disciples, "Assuredly, I say to you that it is hard for a rich man to enter the kingdom of heaven" (Matthew 19:21-23).

I read the passage and realized that the rich young man who had come to the Lord ended up walking away because he thought *the price was too great to pay.* Then the Lord spoke to my heart and said, "Are you going to be the same way?" I said, "No, Sir," and immediately received the Lord Jesus as my Savior, breaking untold generations of strict family tradition and devotion to Hinduism.

I moved closer to my experience with Stevie when I moved from East Africa to the United States and attended Bible school at a Christian university. I earned my bachelor's degree there and then went on to graduate school. I have to confess that I was proud of my intellect. I was intent on earning my Ph.D. in literature, and I liked being "an intellectual." I was faithfully learning to make simple things complicated.

In the midst of my diligent pursuit of intellectual achievement and self-worth through graduate studies, I received the news that my mother was dying of terminal bone cancer in London, where the rest of my family had moved from East Africa. My mother's doctors said that she was going to die in just a few weeks because she had a fast-moving and untreatable form of bone cancer that was eating up her body.

I HAD COME TO THE END OF MYSELF

I didn't have answers for myself or my mother, but she was dying and was asking for me. I was just a poor graduate student in Texas, and I didn't have money to go to England. It just broke me. I had come to the end of myself, and all I could do was weep uncontrollably. Finally, after three days of tears and sorrow, I had an unusual experience on the third night.

Again I went to sleep, and I was taken to that same place I had seen years before when I saw streets of gold. This time I found myself in a grassy place kneeling before the feet of Jesus. I was looking into His face with my hands clasped before me, and I was singing to Him. Jesus had laid His hands on my shoulders, and I was surprised to realize that I was singing to Him in a language I could not understand. Then I woke up, and I knew something had happened. When I felt the urge to pray, I obeyed and said, "Jesus." In that moment, a wind came into my room and took my breath away. Then I felt something bubbling up inside me. When I tried to open my mouth, a song suddenly came out in a language I could not understand! The intellectual part of me said, "This is weird," but the rest of me said, "This may be weird, but this is the most wonderful thing I've ever felt!"

I just kept singing in this strange language for an hour and a half. The only spiritual person I knew at that time was a Catholic nun I'd met in graduate school. I just couldn't wait to talk to somebody about what had happened to me, so I ran to find Sister Marsha. I said, "Sister Marsha, let me tell you what happened to me today!" After I told her about my experience, I asked, "Am I going crazy?" I'll never forget her answer. She put her books down and looked at me with joy and said, "Praise the Lord, brother. You've been baptized in the Holy Ghost!"

The Holy Ghost became very real to me from that day on. He started speaking to me and I quickly realized that He is a *Person*. He started telling me about Jesus. He said, "*Jesus is the same yesterday, today, and forever.*" I hadn't read these words in Hebrews 13:8 yet, so I said, "Huh?" He said, "Jesus is the same yesterday, today, and forever."

PRAY FOR YOUR MOTHER!

This time I said, "Yes." Once again He said, "*Jesus is the same yesterday, today, and forever.*" Finally I said, "Lord, what are You trying to tell me?" He said, "Jesus healed 2,000 years ago. He *still* heals today." When I asked, "What do You mean, Lord?" He said, "Pray for your mother!"

Since I didn't know any better (I hadn't been taught yet that healing isn't for today), I prayed for her as I was told. A few days later I received the news that my mother had been totally healed of her terminal disease! My mother lived another 24 years after that healing and received Jesus Christ before she died.

When I received the baptism of the Holy Ghost, He began to *lead* me.[4] That was when I was led to Lubbock, Texas, where I met Stevie and many other precious children who were in great need of God's love and power. The truth about fasting I learned there became a living word for me since that day. I started observing several 1-day fasts in 1971. In 1972, I began to observe several 3-day fasts over several weeks and then completed some 7-day and 14-day fasts. By 1973, I was conducting several 7-day, 14-day, and 21-day fasts at the instruction of the Lord. During this season the Lord was teaching me *"the unforced rhythms of grace"* that come when we submit our lives completely to His leading. Fasting is an empowerment meant to further the effects of "resting" in the Lord.[5] It should not become an onerous yoke of labor. As you embark on this journey, let me encourage you to find your "rhythm of grace" balanced with the humbling of your soul, wisdom, and obedience. If you are pregnant, nursing or have a medical condition, I recommend that you consult your medical provider before beginning a fast.

Now Go on Two 40-Day Fasts!

In 1974, I was pastoring a church in Levelland, Texas, when the Lord spoke to me and said, "Go on a 40-day fast." I went on a 40-day fast, and I found grace most of the time. The following year, I again conducted a 40-day fast along with several 14-day and 21-day fasts. Bonnie and I married in 1976, and it was that year that the Lord told me, "Now go on two 40-day fasts." For several years after that I observed *two* 40-day fasts per year and a minimum of two 21-day fasts.

I followed this pattern of conducting two 40-day fasts every year after that through 1988, with additional fasts of differing length as the Spirit led. In 1989, I was led to conduct only one 40-day fast. Altogether, I was led by the Spirit to observe 30 separate 40-day fasts. For the first 19, I limited my intake to water only. After that, the Lord allowed me to drink juices. Overall I fasted an average of 120 days per year during that foundational period in my life and ministry!

I did not fully understand what the Lord was doing in those years, but I knew that I loved Jesus. I also knew that He had asked me to fast and pray for His people whom He loved. All I wanted to do was obey. Those who knew me or were closely associated with me as a pastor or leader in those days knew about the fasts, but for more than a decade I was not permitted by the Lord to publicly announce, explain, or teach about my fasting disciplines in public meetings. The Lord was setting a deep foundation during those years. He was doing a secret thing that has only recently been brought into the open at the Lord's command, and this seems to be the way of fasting in most cases.

The Lord desires to draw us into the intimate place of fasting where He can develop our interior life while we are still engaged in the exterior community of regular life.

Not Everyone Understood

I quickly discovered that not everyone understood or accepted what I was doing. There were some who accused me of being a fanatic, and others simply thought that I was overly religious. My worst critics thought that I was self-righteous, and I have to admit that the criticism and misunderstanding were painful at times. Sometimes it is inevitable that obedience to these divine imperatives will create opposition—even among the brethren. Most of the time it is because the enemy of our souls will go to any length to stir up opposition to activities that seriously threaten his dark kingdom. When you are doing spiritual warfare through prayer, praise, worship, intercession, and fasting, the enemy will come to raise up supernatural hindrances and put obstacles in your path.

In the years and decades that have passed since God revealed the secret power of fasting to me in young Stevie's deliverance, that revelation has become a living word and foundation stone in my life and ministry in Christ. Now I understand that God has given me a mandate to help restore this truth about fasting to His end-time Church. Fasting is an extremely important aspect of the New Testament lifestyle of the end-time Church. God asked me to conduct 30 40-day fasts because of the fundamental truth that *you cannot impart something that you do not have.* If you live it, you can give it.

Eventually the Lord said to me, "Now as I have put this in you, I give you the authority to impart this truth to the end-time Church—*to the men and women who are going to do the works of Jesus Christ.*" As I write these words, I feel a sense of destiny and of eternal fulfillment. This book is part of the fruit from the seed sown during all those years of obscurity when all I knew was that I was just obeying a word from the Lord.

God may never ask you to fast for 40 days; although if He does, you *will* be able to do it through His grace. But this fact is clear and beyond dispute: As members in particular of the Church of Jesus Christ, God wants each one of us to observe a certain measure of disciplined fasting in our lives. It is an indispensable part of our lives as members of the Lord's fruit-bearing vine and glorious Bride, and it was a way of life for our ultimate model, Jesus Christ.

ENDNOTES

1. See Psalm 27:10.

2. As is standard for ethical propriety to safeguard the privacy of persons I worked with, I have changed the name of this young man.

3. John 8:32.

4. According to Romans 8:14, this should be happening to you as well!

5. *"Are you tired? Worn out? Burned out on religion? Come to me. Get away with me and you'll recover your life. I'll show you how to take a real rest. Walk with me and work with me—watch how I do it. Learn the unforced rhythms of grace. I won't lay anything heavy or ill-fitting on you. Keep company with Me and you'll learn to live freely and lightly"* (Matthew 11:28-30, Message Bible).

Jesus Is Our Ultimate Model

Jesus upended the lives of His disciples the day He appeared to them shortly after His resurrection as they huddled in fear behind locked doors. He said, *"As the Father has sent Me, I also send you"* (John 20:21b). We would like to think that this is a nice Scripture passage to read instead of what it really is—a timeless call to *follow* Him into the world with the good news.

"As the Father has sent Me, I also send you" (John 20:21b).

This is the Lord's Word to every disciple who hears His voice. Are you His disciple? Do you want to be His disciple? Then say with me right where you are, "As the Father sent Jesus, *Jesus is sending me!*" Jesus is our ultimate model in life, in faith, and in ministry. According to Him, you and I are called and anointed to follow in His footsteps as "sent ones" into the world.

Sometimes I get somewhat irritated by people who don't have the whole picture of God's love for the lost. You don't have to be God to read God's Word and capture at least a hint of the vastness of His love for fallen mankind. When we talk about taking the nations and saving hundreds of millions of souls in Jesus' name, they say, "You are grandiose. You are impractical." Yet this is God's desire. Who would have thought that at the time of this writing, our television broadcasts would be touching over 800 million households per week with the saving message of Jesus Christ and the evidence of the power of the Holy Spirit. This is only the beginning as He gives us the grace to expand our broadcast to more and more nations around the globe.

I'm sure it would have sounded rather grandiose if Jesus had told the disciples hiding in that locked room, "You are going to change the world and reshape history—even the history of the Roman empire and other Gentile nations of which you have never heard," but it was true nevertheless. The *facts* are that Jesus was sending them—and He is sending you and me—just as the Father had sent Him. After that momentous meeting between the risen Lord and His frightened disciples, an anointed army went forth that was full of the Holy Ghost. It moved relentlessly from city to city and nation to nation, proclaiming the Gospel that changed the destiny of humanity and transformed lives wherever they went. That army is about to rise up again!

Jesus was sent *to do a job*. He, as our ultimate model and guide, has imparted that same vision, authority, and responsibility to us! As you and I receive the good news of Jesus in our lives, we are transformed into supernatural shapers of history. We can change the destiny of our churches, our cities, our nation, and even other nations around the world through our obedience to the vision Jesus had—*but it will take the power of God*. The secret to God's power is also found in the commissioning words of Jesus:

Most assuredly, I say to you, he who believes in Me, the works that I do he will do also; and greater works than these he will do, because I go to My Father. And whatever you ask in My name, that I will do, that the Father may be glorified in the Son (John 14:12-13).

Jesus did *not* limit that statement to people who believed in Him in the first century, or to male, Orthodox Jews. It doesn't matter what century you live in, the sole criterion for doing the works that He did is this: Do you believe in Him?

I praise God for Billy Graham, for Charles Finney, John Wesley, and Martin Luther, but they are not our ultimate models for life and ministry. That honor and name is reserved solely for Jesus Christ—and I know that these men would agree. If I do nothing else in these pages, I want to point you to the ultimate model for your life, your calling, and your ministry: Jesus Christ.

HIDING FROM THE WORLD

Although Jesus Christ had invested three long years of His life in the training and instruction of the disciples, they were heartbroken when Jesus gave up His life on the Cross. They buried their leader and did their best to vanish from sight, and their hopes seemed to be sealed in the tomb with Jesus. The problem was that they didn't understand what was really happening in the spirit realm, and they had no idea that they were destined to play a supernatural role in the establishment of the supernatural Church. Their Teacher wasn't finished with them yet. "*Then, the same day at evening, being the first day of the week, when the doors were shut where the disciples were assembled, for fear of the Jews, Jesus came and stood in the midst, and said to them, 'Peace be with you'*" (John 20:19).

We shouldn't judge the disciples of Jesus too harshly for locking themselves away from the outside world. *We are in the same place today!* The modern Church, for the most part, has hidden itself away from the hurting and broken world, following a centuries-old pattern of isolation. Why? I think it is because we have just enough of God's life in us to survive and maintain our lifestyles, but not enough to venture out boldly into the world as ministers to the hurting (like Jesus).

The early disciples went into "survival mode" after Jesus left their sight because they underestimated the power of God and the fullness of His plan. They were thinking, "*They killed our master; they're going to kill us too,*" because they had a wrong perspective of who Jesus was. They were looking at Him as a man who had died instead of the God-Man who would rise again, so naturally they didn't understand who they were or what their destiny was in Christ. No one had any idea that God intended to change the history of the world through that small group of frightened men and women who were hiding away behind locked doors.

The people in that room had already tasted a measure of Christ's authority when He sent them out to heal the sick and cast out devils back in the "good old days." But they didn't feel very strong or authoritative that day in Jerusalem when the resurrected

Jesus walked into the middle of their huddle and turned their world upside down again.

WE HEARD YOU PREACHING!

Several years ago, I was holding an evangelistic outreach in Costa Rica, and we were seeing some wonderful miracles take place in the meetings as God's Spirit confirmed the Word that was preached. It was made even better by the fact that the meetings were broadcast all over Nicaragua, Panama, and Costa Rica. On the third day of the outreach, Bonnie flew in with our two eldest children. When they arrived at the airport, the radio broadcast of my service was being played over the airport public address system. The first thing they heard upon landing was the sound of my preaching.

I'll never forget the moment my son ran up to me that day with his face beaming with joy and pride. He said, "Daddy, when we came to the airport we heard you preaching!" It blessed me to see my son get so excited about souls. He has always had a soft heart for missions, and even to this day I put my hands on Ben and pray a prayer that echoes the heart of Jesus toward us: "Lord, if You tarry, I pray that Ben will *see greater things* and *do greater things* than I have done." That is the heart of loving mothers and fathers, isn't it? The Father always wants the double portion for His sons and daughters. I would never tell any of my children, "Don't you do better than I!" No, my heart is to see every one of my children do *better* than Bonnie and I have done.

Jesus revealed our heavenly Father's heart when He said, "...*the works that I do* [you] *will do also; and greater works than these* [you] *will do, because I go to My Father*" (John 14:12b). This is the encouragement, the heavenly vision, the timely Word of the Lord for our generation! If we are approaching the end of the endtimes and the coming of the Lord, then this Word must be fulfilled quickly. If Jesus is going to come soon, this divine promise must be fulfilled first. I am confessing that we will see the "greater works" in this generation!

WHAT ARE THE "WORKS" OF JESUS?

Since Jesus is our model, and since we are ordained to do those same works and even exceed them, then we need to look at these works to learn what is in store for us in the days ahead. The fourth chapter of the Gospel of Luke reveals the first work of Jesus: He is filled with the anointing of the Holy Spirit.

> *Then Jesus, being filled with the Holy Spirit, returned from the Jordan and was led by the Spirit into the wilderness, being tempted for forty days by the devil. And in those days He ate nothing, and afterward, when they had ended, He was hungry (Luke 4:1-2).*

The Bible says that Jesus was hungry, but it says nothing about Him being thirsty. So in other words, Jesus fasted for 40 days, drinking only water. It is important for you to notice one particular phrase in the Bible record: "*...being **filled with the Holy Spirit**....*" Jesus was full of the Holy Spirit before He was driven by the Spirit into the wilderness. Secondly, He *fasts* for 40 days while being tempted. Finally, He concludes His wilderness season in a confrontation with the devil that is recorded in Luke 4 and elsewhere.

Satan came to tempt Jesus with the three great temptations he has always used on man:

1. First he questioned the Lord's identity as the Son of God and tempted Him to use His power for selfish purposes by turning a stone into bread to satisfy His hunger.

2. Then the devil tempted the Lord to grasp the authority and glory of all the kingdoms of the earth—or take a devilish shortcut to the "top"—if He would only worship the devil.

3. Finally, the devil again questioned the Lord's identity and used Scripture quoted out of context to entice Him to throw His life down and trust in the angels to save Him—again for the self-serving purpose of "proving something." Jesus defeated the tempter every time using the Word of God, saying, "It is written...."

These three temptations surfaced again during the three years Jesus ministered among men. He was challenged to summon rescuing angels when He was on the Cross to prove who He was—an act that would have aborted His mission of redemption. He was also tempted by the crowds to seize the throne and become Israel's political savior instead of their spiritual Redeemer. Finally, the mocking challenge to Jesus to summon angels while He was on the Cross was also a rehash of satan's third temptation for Jesus to throw His life down and *trust angels to save it*. Jesus willingly laid His life down, but not for Himself. And He refused to be saved from death—He intended to swallow it up and destroy it forever, in perfect obedience to His Father's will.

THE SECRET OF HIS POWER

How could Jesus do these things and accomplish the astounding miracles we see throughout the four Gospels? The secret of His power is found in Luke 4:14: "*Then Jesus returned in the power of the Spirit to Galilee, and news of Him went out through all the surrounding region.*"

Look carefully at the difference between verses 1 and 14 of Luke chapter 4: Before the temptation in the wilderness, the Bible says that Jesus was *filled with the Spirit.* That is a good thing, but look at verse 14. At the end of the wilderness temptation and 40 days of fasting, Jesus had totally defeated satan and came out of that experience *in the power of the Spirit!* He was led of the Holy Spirit into the wilderness to be tested. As He obeyed, under the unction of the Holy Spirit, He became empowered to pull down satanic strongholds. So there is a clear difference between being *filled* with the Spirit and operating in the *power* of the Spirit! Something transformed Jesus from being a "Spirit-filled" man into a man who walked in the "power" of the Spirit. Remember that Christ was fully God and fully man. His example in fasting provides God's insight into dealing with obstacles of both flesh and spirit. We need to make the secret of Jesus' power the secret of *our power,* because He is, after all, our ultimate model.

This is the same secret I discovered in my wilderness experience while working with Stevie and the other children in Lubbock, Texas. This is where God wants all of us to move. Many of us function at the level of being filled with the Spirit, and I firmly believe that the in-filling of the Holy Spirit is wonderful.

But it is only the first stage of progression beyond salvation. We need to go on.

MOVE BEYOND THE IN-FILLING INTO THE POWER OF THE SPIRIT

Jesus Christ showed us the way and personally modeled it for us. Being filled with the Spirit does not make you ready to move into the fullness of your calling in power. We need to submit to the discipline of the Holy Spirit, and during that time frame God will disciple us in the crucial works of prayer, fasting, and the skillful use of His Word as a weapon. *Then* we will go forth in the *power* of the Spirit to do God's will.

We have majored on the Word of God for centuries and have learned some things along the way. We are just beginning to step into obedience regarding the discipline of prayer today, but fasting remains a rarely practiced mystery to the modern Church. It is here that we find the principal key to going beyond the in-filling of the Spirit to tap the *power* of the Spirit.

Jesus fully completed the process in only 40 days, but it would probably take you and me much longer. The important point here is to *begin*. The disciples were with Jesus for three years, during which time they were discipled under the anointing of Jesus Christ. Yet it was only after the wilderness of the crucifixion and the time of fasting and prayer in the upper room that they pressed through and received both the *in-filling* of the Holy Spirit and the *dunamis* or "power" of the Spirit to boldly proclaim the Gospel in the face of opposition.

I want you to see that fasting helps release the power of the Spirit in our lives. It doesn't necessarily help you "earn" more grace from God, but it facilitates the freer flow of the Holy Spirit through you by dissolving and removing all the junk in your life. This can only be accomplished through times of fasting and prayer.

If you give yourself to the Lord in a life that's committed to prayer and to fasting, His anointing will begin to flow through you in greater and greater power. These things are the "first works" we are called to do if we want to do the works of Jesus Christ. The initial or first work of Jesus before He went into His ministry in the *power* of the Spirit was to fast and wage spiritual warfare in prayer and the Word.

I don't believe in accidents in the Kingdom. It is no accident that you are reading these words. I believe that you were led to this point by the Holy Spirit because you are one of the people He has chosen to serve in His end-time army—you are called and anointed *to do the works of Jesus Christ*, and even *greater* works!

You don't have to go on dramatically long fasts to get the benefits of fasting and spiritual warfare. The critical element is not the length of the fast, but that you yield to His leading. I've noticed that God always raises up certain men and women to personally live out certain truths to extreme depths so they can speak and teach them to others with proven authority. That is what happened to me. God released me to teach authoritatively about prayer and fasting, but only after I had quietly conducted many lengthy fasts over a period of two decades at a certain cost to myself and my family. God is not interested in teaching "theory," but in imparting spiritual truths backed up by solid *personal experience and application* of His Word. God gives us such people as *examples* to encourage us to press into Him in certain areas of importance to His plans and purposes for our lives. He wants you to measure up to *His* purpose for your life.

The difference between the *anointing* of the Spirit and the *power* of the Spirit is dramatically illustrated in the incident described in chapter 17 of the Gospel of Matthew following Jesus' transfiguration on the mountain:

> *And when they had come to the multitude, a man came to Him, kneeling down to Him and saying, "Lord, have mercy on my son, for he is an epileptic and suffers severely; for he often falls into the fire and often into the water. So I brought him to Your disciples, but they could not cure him." Then Jesus answered and said, "O faithless and perverse generation, how long shall I be with you? How long shall I bear with you? Bring him here to Me." And Jesus rebuked the demon, and it came out of him; and the child was cured from that very hour. Then the disciples came to Jesus privately and said, "Why could we not cast it out?" So Jesus said to them, "Because of your unbelief; for assuredly, I say to you, if you have faith as a mustard seed, you will say to this mountain, 'Move from here to there,' and it will move; and nothing will be impossible for you. However, this kind does not go out except by prayer and fasting"* (Matthew 17:14-21).

The reason Jesus was so stern with His disciples was because He had already given them His authority (or *anointing*) as delegated representatives of the Kingdom in Matthew chapter 10. He said, *"Heal the sick, cleanse the lepers, raise the dead, cast out demons. Freely you have received, freely give"* (Matt. 10:8).

The disciples had enjoyed success during an extensive tour of ministry, but they suddenly hit rock bottom in Matthew 17 when they encountered an evil spirit that refused to yield to the delegated authority the disciples had. When it got down to the "nitty gritty" of extreme spiritual warfare, the disciples prayed for this little boy, but were openly defeated because they didn't have the power to overcome the demon controlling the child. Something prevented them. Some force or power was hindering the healing. There was a dark oppression in that little boy that had *completely undermined and discredited the anointing* possessed by the Lord's disciples! The credibility of their ministry had been totally compromised by the time Jesus arrived on the scene. What was it? The boy's father said his son was afflicted with epilepsy, but in any case, Jesus didn't heal the boy; He cast out the demon that was causing the affliction.[1]

When Jesus was alone with the disciples, He gave them one of the most important keys believers can ever learn to win victory against the greatest obstructions the enemy places in our lives, ministries, and callings. This key can only be perceived and received in the realm of the Spirit because our victory lies in the realm of the Spirit. God has given us mighty weapons for the "pulling down of strongholds" according to the apostle Paul:

> *For though we walk in the flesh, we do not war according to the flesh. For the weapons of our warfare are not carnal but mighty in God for pulling down strongholds, casting*

down arguments and every high thing that exalts itself against the knowledge of God, bringing every thought into captivity to the obedience of Christ, and being ready to punish all disobedience when your obedience is fulfilled (2 Corinthians 10:3-6).

Since our weapons (and therefore our victory) are not found in the natural realm of "flesh and blood," our enemy, the devil, will try as often as he can to get us into the natural or fleshly mode of battle and struggle. The most effective way for you and me to put our flesh in its place and walk in the Spirit is to *fast and pray*. If the Son of God fasted and prayed for *power* in His ministry, why should you and I think we are exempt from these things?

When You Pray...

Jesus expects you to fast and to pray. In Matthew 6:5-7, He didn't say, "When you *feel like praying*...." No, He said three times, "**When you pray**...." Not *if*.

In the same way, Jesus didn't say, "If you should someday decide to *try to fast*, although I know it's almost impossible for you..." in Matthew 6:16-17. No, He said, "*When you fast*...." He didn't give us the option not to fast. He considered it to be such a natural part of the Christian life that He told the disciples *and their critics* that prayer and fasting would be a part of their lives after He left them. *Nothing has changed since He said those words.* If you are a Christian, then you pray. If you are a Christian, then you fast.

God wants to release a double anointing in us so that we can bring that authoritative word of healing, deliverance, and restoration that the disciples witnessed in the deliverance of the epileptic boy. The disciples later exercised that same demon-busting power of the Spirit in the Book of Acts and throughout the narratives of the Epistles. It is about time for us to do the world-changing *works of Jesus* as we see the devastation in the world around us!

In the Book of Joel, the Lord had the prophet summon the elders, the adult inhabitants, the children, the nursing infants, and even the bride and bridegroom waiting for their marriage ceremony to observe a solemn fast as one nation before God. Why and for what? They prayed urgently that *restoration* would come (see Joel 2:15ff). God answered their prayer with a great promise concerning the last days that only began to be fulfilled on the Day of Pentecost in the Book of Acts and is being manifested as never before in our day:

> *And it shall come to pass afterward that I will pour out My Spirit on all flesh; your sons and your daughters shall prophesy, your old men shall dream dreams, your young men shall see visions. And also on My menservants and on My maidservants I will pour out My Spirit in those days* (Joel 2:28-29).

The only precondition for this Holy Spirit outpouring is that we be a people who will see the vision and that we be willing to pay the price for power through prayer and fasting.

If the Holy Spirit has stirred you as you read through this chapter, then God is probably preparing you for war! He has chosen you to *do the works of Jesus* in your generation, and that can only be done *in the power of the Spirit*. If you are willing to take up the supernatural weapon of prayer and fasting as a regular part of your arsenal, then say to the Lord right now, "As You lead, Lord Jesus." If you are willing to pay the price of regular prayer and fasting so that you can pull down strongholds, have victory for your life, and bring deliverance and freedom to the captives in your generation, then tell the Lord, "Where You lead me, Lord, I will follow."

He may lead you to fast one day per month, one day per week, or simply one day every two months. Whatever it is, commit yourself to do it and trust the Lord for the grace to obey. If you pastor a congregation, then you may be led by the Lord to lead your church body into seasons of corporate fasting. It is important to lay your life down before Him today and trust Him for tomorrow.

Your obedient response to God is at the same time one of the most feared and dangerous catastrophes that could befall the kingdom of darkness. The enemy knows that you can change the shape and the destiny of your city and even your nation by joining God's end-time army of men and women who are committed to fasting and prayer. The Lord has given me a visionary prayer concerning His work among the members of His end-time army of believers:

"Lord God, I see Your angels equipping these armies with mighty weapons of warfare. I see troops of men and women in different ranks who are putting Your weapons in their arsenal. Let the anointing come now, Lord. Let the double portion of Your Holy Spirit come and touch us.

"Let Your sons and daughters receive anointing and grace to fast and pray. And may the anointing that I have received be imparted to the one reading these words and praying this prayer with me right now.

"I see this army marching, Lord. We are marching to take the cities for Jesus! We are marching to take the Lord's name to every realm and to every corner of the earth—east, west, north, and south. The army of God is advancing and every demon must bow to the name of Jesus as the anointed army comes with Your mighty weapons of warfare. Lord God, we commit ourselves this day to use these weapons faithfully. Lord, I pray that the pastors and leaders in Your army will see that they are generals in the army of God. Place within them, Lord God, the divine wisdom they need to lead their portion of the army into victory. Thank You for total victory, Lord Jesus."

Now we will go on to discover the incredible benefits we receive when we obey God in our prayer and fasting.

ENDNOTE

1. This passage in Matthew 17:14-21 speaks of a specific instance in which the outward manifestation of epilepsy (so named by the boy's father) was actually caused by the presence of an evil spirit. Not all cases of epilepsy are caused by the presence of evil spirits, but some are. It takes the discernment of the Holy Spirit to know when to pray for healing of the disease of epilepsy (caused by physical damage or abnormalities in the brain or nervous system), and when to cast out the demonic force causing such seizure activity.

The Life-Changing Benefits of Fasting

Nearly every Christian I have talked with has had some questions and misconceptions about fasting. I think it is sadly safe to say that fasting is one of the most misunderstood subjects in the Bible. There are incredible benefits you receive through fasting according to God's Word. Twelve specific benefits of the "fast that God has chosen" are listed in the Book of Isaiah:

Is this not the fast that I have chosen: to loose the bonds of wickedness, to undo the heavy burdens, to let the oppressed go free, and that you break every yoke? Is it not to share your bread with the hungry, and that you bring to your house the poor who are cast out; when you see the naked, that you cover him, and not hide yourself from your own flesh? Then your light shall break forth like the morning, your healing shall spring forth speedily, and your righteousness shall go before you; the glory of the Lord shall be your rear guard. Then you shall call, and the Lord will answer;

you shall cry, and He will say, "Here I am." If you take away the yoke from your midst, the pointing of the finger, and speaking wickedness, If you extend your soul to the hungry and satisfy the afflicted soul, then your light shall dawn in the darkness, and your darkness shall be as the noonday. The Lord will guide you continually, and satisfy your soul in drought, and strengthen your bones; you shall be like a watered garden, and like a spring of water, whose waters do not fail. Those from among you shall build the old waste places; you shall raise up the foundations of many generations; and you shall be called the Repairer of the Breach, the Restorer of Streets to Dwell In (Isaiah 58:6-12).

Isaiah 58 is one of the best chapters in the Bible on the subject of fasting. I could stay on this passage for several chapters or an entire book! It is wonderful. There are at least 12 specific benefits of "the fast that God has chosen" listed in this passage:

1. Revelation

2. Healing and wholeness

3. Righteousness

4. The presence of the *shekinah* glory of God

5. Answered prayers

6. Continual guidance

7. Contentment

8. Refreshing

9. Strength

10. Work that endures (like an ever-flowing spring)

11. Raising up of future generations

12. Restoration

How does fasting *really* work? I don't know all the answers because this is one of God's great mysteries, but I can share what I've learned up to this point. For one thing, demons get very uncomfortable when Christians begin fasting. We know from the Scriptures that many of the diseases, ailments, mental problems, and chronic behavioral problems afflicting humanity are instigated or perpetuated by demonic forces who want to hinder God's people and generally torment God's highest creation.

I often recommend to people who are seeking a healing from the Lord that they fast before they come to our healing services. Those who heed this advice often receive a supernatural healing from the Lord very quickly. I tell people, "If your loved one comes to services, have them fast beforehand. Ask them to drink fruit or vegetable juices, or to get by on salad." The observation of some kind of fast is important because it shows a desperation and determination to "touch the Lord," who alone is the source of all healing. Demons cannot stay around too long when a person fasts, because fasting unto God creates a totally different atmosphere that welcomes the holy and repels the unholy. That is why demonic spirits get very uncomfortable around a person who fasts.

Any pastor or minister who is in a healing and deliverance ministry of any kind should make fasting part of his regular lifestyle. It is the spiritual equivalent of an athlete working out at the gym. As you fast and seek God's face, He will begin to plant an authority in you born out of intimacy with Him that the demons will recognize and fear.

Early in my ministry, I remember receiving a phone call from two Pentecostal pastors. They said, "Brother Mahesh, we're in trouble. We were praying for a man who is a homosexual, and suddenly he began speaking in a very strange voice, saying that he wanted to have fellowship with us. We can sense evil here, and we are afraid. Please come help us." "You are men of God," I said, "You have authority. Just cast the demon out of him." But again they told me that they were afraid. "But you are pastors," I said. The men persisted, saying, "Please, Brother Mahesh, we need your help." Finally I agreed to go.

They gave me the directions to the house and instructed me, "Please come in the back door." I drove to their location and walked into the kitchen. I could hear some muffled sounds from behind a door. When I went to investigate, I found these two pastors were hiding in the broom closet! "What are you doing here?" I asked. They simply motioned toward the front of the house and said, "*He's out there!*"

The moment I entered the room where the young man was, I could feel the powers of darkness. A demon had manifested in this man, and it was a strong one. I had been fasting, and when I went into the room, the man was standing there as if waiting for a chance to intimidate again. As soon as I looked at him, I saw something looking back at me, something in his eyes that was not him. A different personality was present, an evil and demonic one. I could see that the demon had come to the surface. He was literally staring out of the man. You could see it because the man's whole countenance had been transformed into a mask of evil. He saw me and said in an incredibly evil tone, "Oh, *another man*. Come in, I'd like to have fellowship with you." Now it was my turn to do the talking by the power of the Holy Spirit.

"You want to have fellowship with me? Do you know what the Scriptures say? '…if we walk in the light as He is in the light, we have *fellowship* with one another, and the *blood of Jesus Christ* cleanses us from all sin.'[1]

"Now demon, can you say, 'The blood of Jesus'?" The thing could only growl at this point. The arrogant tone disappeared instantly. "Demon, say 'the blood of Jesus' now! Come on!"

The man's hands started twisting, and I could literally hear bones cracking. Then the man's ankles began to twist in a contorted manner, and he fell on the floor and started writhing. I said, "Stop doing that. Say, 'the blood of Jesus.' Say it now!" Finally he went, "The bl—, the bl—." Then the man seemed to regurgitate, and the demon came out screaming.

I returned to that area years later, and a man knocked on my hotel door. I remembered his face, but the last time I had seen the man, he was lying on the floor while two ministers huddled in a broom closet in another room. This time, he said, "Brother Chavda, I want to introduce you to someone." He stepped aside so I could see the young lady who was with him and he said, "We have been married for five years, and I want you to know that when you prayed for me that day, *I was totally delivered* from homosexual desires." Praise God! Jesus is the great Deliverer.

Another time I was ministering in the morning service of a church in a university town in the Southwest. I had just come through a season of fasting and prayer, and the services were going very well in the large church building. The altar was so large that it could accommodate hundreds of people at once, and I felt like the Lord wanted to bless the *whole audience* at once, so I brought them all up to the altar. As the Lord anointed the people, many were falling or responding to God's presence in different ways. Right in the middle of the altar service, the Spirit of God prompted me to say, "The Lord tells me there are twelve homosexuals and lesbians here. If you'll raise your hands and repent right now, the Lord will deliver each one of you."

Twelve hands went up instantly. Eight of the people were lesbians, and when they raised their hands it looked like they were suddenly dropped to the floor by a blow from a large hammer! I knew the Lord wanted to do more, so I went down to where they lay on the carpet. I didn't know much about lesbians. I thought they all had men's haircuts and wore jeans and bossed everybody around. One particular young woman had confessed that she was a lesbian, but she defied the usual stereotype. She was a beautiful 21-year-old blonde-haired little girl, but when I looked at her, her entire visage turned dark.

I told her, "You are being delivered from a demon of death. In fact, it is a spirit of suicide. You tried to commit suicide just recently, haven't you?" She started weeping and pulled up the sleeves of her long-sleeved dress to show me the vivid scars from the day only two weeks earlier when she had slashed her wrists in an attempt to commit suicide. Right then and there, under the overpowering anointing of God, that young woman was totally delivered from the spirit of suicide and the spirit of lesbianism.

When I went back to that church a year later, I rejoiced to see that this sister was playing a key role on the worship team. She came up to me with a big smile and proudly pulled out a picture and said, "I just want you to know that I got married three weeks ago, and this is the man I married. Now I'm serving the Lord!"

I want you to see the people who are in bondage all around you. They are broken, hurting, and desperate under demonizing influences. Psychologists cannot help them, nor can psychiatrists. God's Word says that this kind won't even come out by a simple command in the name of Jesus Christ—they do not come out except through prayer and fasting. That, my friend, is what the Lord is asking us to do. Are you willing to pay the price to set the captives free? Are you willing to set the captives free in your church, in your neighborhood, and in your city?

We shouldn't be satisfied to stop there. There are desperately wicked yokes of bondage and evil regimes choking the people of the nations. I want the Church of Jesus Christ to rise up in God's glory. I'm tired of seeing Christians tear one another down when there are so many desperate needs out in the world. We are called to set the captives free, and the Lord has given us mighty weapons to pull down the strongholds.

Everyone seeking deliverance from an entangling sin or chronic weakness needs to get desperate. If parents want to see their children healed or set free of demonic oppression, then they need to get desperate for their children. If they are truly humble and desperate before the Lord as they fast for themselves or for their children, then they will often find that it becomes easy to experience or minister deliverance. They may well experience what I experienced the first time with little Stevie.

WHY DO WE FAST?

I've compiled a list of nine biblical reasons why we fast, and they don't necessarily parallel the list of 12 benefits of fasting listed in Isaiah 58. Many of these points get down to the "nitty gritty" areas of the Christian life, and they answer some of the most common questions I've been asked about fasting over the last two decades.

1. *We fast in obedience to God's Word.*

Fasting is deeply embedded in God's Word. It is a tool of overcoming leaders in both the Old and New Testaments. If the Bible record is any indication, then "Winners fast and losers don't." Here is a very brief sampling of what God has to say to believers, and ministers in particular, about fasting:

"Now, therefore," says the Lord, "turn to Me with all your heart, with fasting, with weeping, and with mourning" (Joel 2:12).

But in all things we commend ourselves as ministers of God: in much patience, in tribulations, in needs, in distresses, in stripes, in imprisonments, in tumults, in labors, in sleeplessness, in fastings; by purity, by knowledge, by longsuffering, by kindness, by the Holy Spirit, by sincere love (2 Corinthians 6:4-6).

And Jesus said to them, "Can the friends of the bridegroom mourn as long as the bridegroom is with them? But the days will come when the bridegroom will be taken away from them, and then they will fast" (Matthew 9:15).

2. *We fast to humble ourselves before God and obtain His grace and power.*

How often do you need grace? Do you need to tap into God's power to accomplish the callings and vision He has placed in your heart? We all need His continuous power to live the victorious Christian life daily. So would it hurt to fast at least one day per week to "keep the plugs clean" in your life? Fasting keeps you honest. James the apostle made this point abundantly clear: If you want power and grace from God, then you have to humble yourself: *"Humble yourselves in the sight of the Lord, and He will lift you up"* (James 4:10). The Holy Spirit is called the Spirit of grace. If you want the Spirit of grace, if you want the anointing, you humble yourself. (We will deal with this crucial subject in greater detail in Chapter Five.)

3. *We fast to overcome temptations in areas that keep us from moving into God's power.*

If the anointing is not flowing freely through you, that is a good sign that you need to fast and pray. It is time to clear the channel so God's Spirit can flow through you. Once again, turn to the pattern of the great Pioneer of our faith, Jesus. According to Luke chapter 4, Jesus came out of a wilderness of temptation *in the power of the Spirit.* If you want the same, then do what He did. Jesus ate nothing for 40 days, and afterward the devil came to tempt Him when He was hungry. When Jesus had soundly whipped the devil, He went forth *in power*.

4. *We fast to be purified from sin (and to help others become purified as well).*

According to the Word of God, Jesus Christ took away all the sins of the world on the cross at Calvary. Yet many (if not all) of us have to deal with "besetting" or "entangling" sins that seem to keep popping up again and again. God wants us not only to defeat these entangling sins in our own lives, but also to go beyond our own needs to stand in the gap as intercessors for others. If there is a habit or chronic sin that keeps cropping up in your life, then humble your soul in fasting, and God will purify you. Be prepared, then, for the time the Lord asks you to take upon yourself (through intercession) the sins of others and combine your intercessory prayer with fasting. The great models for this are Jesus Christ and the prophet Daniel:

> *Then I set my face toward the Lord God to make request by prayer and supplications, with fasting, sackcloth, and ashes. And I prayed to the Lord my God, and made confession, and said, "O Lord, great and awesome God, who keeps His covenant and mercy with those who love Him, and with those who keep His commandments, we have sinned and committed iniquity, we have done wickedly and rebelled, even by departing from Your precepts and Your judgments"* (Daniel 9:3-5).

We can pray this great model prayer for ourselves, for our congregation, for our children, and even for our city and nation. It says, "God, we have sinned. We have departed from Your ways,

O God. We are in defeat because of our sins and transgressions." Now remember that the man who was praying these things, Daniel, was the most righteous man in his generation! This was the man who would rather pray than escape the lions' den, yet he said, "God, *we* have sinned."

Many times I've shared this principle with pastors who protested, saying, "You don't understand! We are fine. We are OK. We live godly lives here." I tell them, "Listen, you don't understand! We may be OK, but *our cities* and *our nations* are crumbling! We need to take upon ourselves this burden and say, 'God, we have sinned, we have become lazy. Forgive us and restore us.'"

As believers and intercessors in the pattern of the Great Intercessor, we are called and expected to take upon ourselves the burdens of others. It is simply an unavoidable part of "taking up our cross daily." At times, entire cities or nations fast to repent and be purified from sin. This happened in the days of Jonah. The Ninevites were a wicked and violent people who were about to be judged and annihilated by God, but then *they went on a fast* (even the donkeys, camels, and goats were put on a fast!):

> *So the people of Nineveh believed God, proclaimed a fast, and put on sackcloth, from the greatest to the least of them. Then word came to the king of Nineveh; and he arose from his throne and laid aside his robe, covered himself with sackcloth and sat in ashes. And he caused it to be proclaimed and published throughout Nineveh by the decree of the king and his nobles, saying, Let neither man nor beast, herd nor flock, taste anything; do not let them eat, or*

drink water. But let man and beast be covered with sack-cloth, and cry mightily to God; yes, let every one turn from his evil way and from the violence that is in his hands. Who can tell if God will turn and relent, and turn away from His fierce anger, so that we may not perish? Then God saw their works, that they turned from their evil way; and God relented from the disaster that He had said He would bring upon them, and He did not do it (Jonah 3:5-10).

Nineveh turned to the Living God. They received the Gospel when Thomas came to them. And 3,000 years later, at this writing the only Christian elected to parliament in the first free Iraqi elections was from Nineveh.

Fasting for purity can be pretty confusing at times because of the very nature of the cleansing process. Fasting has a way of bringing every nasty habit and irritation you've got just bubbling to the surface. You will quickly notice—especially on longer fasts—that if you have a bad temper hidden down there where no one else (but God and your spouse) can see, then it will come right to the surface and you'll start roaring at people. Be patient and be encouraged, and don't give up. The Lord will clean you out.

5. *We fast to become weak before God so God's power can be strong.*

Fasting is a choice *for God* and *against the flesh*. When you fast, you are making a conscious inward choice demonstrated by an outward act that you want God's power to flow through you, not your own. You want God's answer, not yours.

Many years ago when I was just beginning to step out in the ministry, I received a call from a couple whom I loved and had prayed for often. I didn't have any money to spare at the time, but my heart went out to this couple when they said, "Brother Mahesh, we are in need." They were both in graduate school at the time and they would have to drop out if they didn't find money for tuition somehow or somewhere.

They told me, "Mahesh, we just want you to be in prayer," but I loved them so much that I said, "Well..." and was about to say that I was going to send them all the money I had in my bank account. I was still taking some courses at the university myself, and I needed what money I had managed to save so I could register for my final series of classes. As they talked, I said to myself, "I'm going to take all that I've saved for registration and give it to them." It was the "arm of the flesh" speaking. There's nothing wrong with giving to those in need, but this time they were calling me *to pray* and I was about to simply send them money instead.

Suddenly God seemed to speak to me in the other ear, "Mahesh, do *you* want to help them or would you rather that *I* help them?" I said, "*You*, Sir," and I prayed for them.

The very next day, both of these people received full scholarships to the university. The miracle of provision didn't stop there! God continued to take care of all their needs supernaturally for the next two years! In contrast, the "weak arm of the flesh of Mahesh" could have helped my friends for about three days at best—if I'd totally emptied my slim bank account. God's way is always best. Consider what God's Word has to say:

My knees are weak through fasting, and my flesh is feeble from lack of fatness. I also have become a reproach to them; when they look at me, they shake their heads. Help me, O Lord my God! Oh, save me according to Your mercy, That they may know that this is Your hand; that You, Lord, have done it! Let them curse, but You bless... (Psalm 109:24-28).

And He said to me, "My grace is sufficient for you, for My strength is made perfect in weakness." Therefore most gladly I will rather boast in my infirmities, that the power of Christ may rest upon me. Therefore I take pleasure in infirmities, in reproaches, in needs, in persecutions, in distresses, for Christ's sake. For when I am weak, then I am strong (2 Corinthians 12:9-10).

I've learned that it is important for us as ministers of God to become completely weak before God. It is at that point that the Lord will send us out in His power.

6. *We fast to release the anointing to accomplish His will.*

The leaders at the church in Antioch fasted and prayed before they sent out Barnabas and Paul. This was done so the leaders would make the right choice, *and* it was done to ensure their success in the Gospel mission. Barnabas and Paul followed the same pattern in the foreign cities where they established churches—they fasted and prayed before appointing elders in those cities. The fasting and prayer helped guide their choices and helped ensure the successful ministry of those elders. They wanted God's grace and anointing to continue in those churches long after the apostles had gone (see Acts 13:3-4; 14:23).

7. *We fast in times of crisis.*

Men have always turned to God in prayer and fasting in times of crisis. The Book of Esther records what was probably the most critical time in the history of the Jewish nation. Even though Hitler brutally massacred six million Jews during World War II in a terrible holocaust, thousands of Jews still survived in other places around the world. In Esther's time, the Jews had not yet been dispersed and Haman was literally on the verge of successfully destroying the *entire* Jewish race! The king of the Persians and Medes had already signed the death warrant when Esther commanded the Jews to observe a fast before she risked her life to enter the king's presence to obtain mercy and pardon for her people.

> *Then Esther told them to reply to Mordecai: "Go, gather all the Jews who are present in Shushan, and fast for me; neither eat nor drink for three days, night or day. My maids and I will fast likewise. And so I will go to the king, which is against the law; and if I perish, I perish!"* (Esther 4:15-16)

In times of crisis, we may need to fast the most aggressive fast of all and totally abstain from food and water. However, I would never counsel you to do that for more than *three days* unless you are in the literal glory and presence of God. This three-day fast is the fast that Esther asked the Jews to observe. In the end, God turned that crisis around and brought deliverance to all the Jews.

Again in Second Chronicles 20, Judah was about to be destroyed by enemies when King Jehoshaphat put the people on a fast. In the end, they witnessed one of the most dramatic acts of supernatural deliverance recorded in the Bible as the angels of God came and wiped out the armies of three invading nations!

8. *We fast when seeking God's direction.*

Then I proclaimed a fast there at the river of Ahava, that we might humble ourselves before our God, to seek from Him the right way for us and our little ones and all our possessions. For I was ashamed to request of the king an escort of soldiers and horsemen to help us against the enemy on the road, because we had spoken to the king, saying, "The hand of our God is upon all those for good who seek Him, but His power and His wrath are against all those who forsake Him." So we fasted and entreated our God for this, and He answered our prayer (Ezra 8:21-23).

When you need God's direction, when you are confused about which way to go, one of the best things you can do is *fast.* This is especially true in the sometimes confusing area of personal relationships, particularly for those believers trying to make a choice about whom to marry. The Lord taught me this principle of fasting before I got married, and I fasted for my wife even though I was not yet married and didn't even know her! I knew that God had not called me to live alone, and I knew that God knew where and who she was; so I fasted and prayed for her. Bonnie and I compared notes later on and discovered that at the most critical time in her life, after her parents got a divorce, she went through some very intense times, I was fasting for her and praying that God would give her deliverance!

9. *We fast for understanding and divine revelation.*

As believers, we need more than direction. We need *revelation* and *understanding* of certain matters, situations, or truths in the Bible. The Bible says, "*You go, therefore, and read from the scroll which you have written at my instruction, the words of the Lord, in the hearing of the people in the Lord's house on the day of fasting...*" (Jer. 36:6).

Sometimes the Lord's revelation doesn't necessarily come at the time of the fast, but later on. This happened to me the time the Lord showed me a *wonderful principle of healing* during a mass evangelistic outreach in Haiti. The meetings were held immediately after the Duvalier regime fell in that nation, and God had given us some wonderful miracles in the services. However, the local voodoo priests and witch doctors had become so disturbed by our services that for the first time ever they issued a nationwide radio broadcast calling for a meeting between all the voodoo priests and practitioners to put curses on us! I said, "Wow, wonderful! Let's see what you can do." (I responded in this way because like Elijah before me, I *knew* God was surrounding us with His glory.)

During this same series of meetings, a certain woman who had been born blind was brought to the front by her granddaughter. Each time this little lady would come to the front with her hand on her granddaughter's shoulder, and I would pray for her. Every time the anointing of God would hit her and she would fall down like I had hit her with all my strength, although I barely touched her. I knew something had happened, but each time I helped her up and asked, "How are you, Grandma?" she would blink her still blind eyes and say, "I can't see." I could only answer, "Okay. Come again."

The same thing happened each service after that for seven days and nights. She would be led forward by her granddaughter. The power of God would hit her, her body would shake, and down she would go. I knew it was the genuine power of the Lord hitting her. It was so obvious that I almost wanted the Lord to be gentle. Yet each time I helped her up again and asked, "How are you?" she would shake her head and say she still couldn't see.

I was really struggling with this situation. As you might imagine, when you are conducting healing services, you don't necessarily want the first people to come up for prayer to be born blind! There's a strong temptation to ask for the warts or headaches first. The Lord doesn't think that way.

By the fourth day, I was getting tired of seeing Grandma coming forward for prayer. Thank God she wasn't looking to me for healing; she was looking to the Lord. Once again, the same thing happened. In fact, the *same thing happened* on the fifth day and the sixth day. She would come forward, I would pray, she would fall down, I would help her up, she would shake her head no, and I would say, "God bless you, come back again," and so on.

On the last service of the last day of the outreach in Haiti, my favorite grandmother came forward to the front once again with her hand on her granddaughter's shoulder. Once again I prayed for her, and again the incredible power of God hit her so hard that she was absolutely knocked to the floor, just like every service before that. Once again I knelt down and said, "God bless you, Grandma," and went on. But this time the Lord said, "Help her up." So I said, "Okay." I went back to help this dear lady to her feet.

Once again I asked her, "How are you, Grandma?" She blinked her eyes and said, "*I can see you clearly!*" God had totally recreated her eyes and given her sight for the first time in her life! Outwardly I exclaimed, "How wonderful!" but inwardly I said, "You know, Lord, You could have done this the first day!"

Many months later during an extended time of fasting and prayer, I was driving down a street in South Florida where I lived at the time. I was minding my own business and wasn't even praying on the eighteenth day of the fast when suddenly, right in front of my eyes, I began to view scenes of the times I had prayed for that precious Haitian grandmother. It was almost as if I was watching a full-color videotape of those prayer times.

I had wondered many times about the seven days I had prayed for that blind woman, and suddenly I found myself reliving those times in living color. Only this time I knew I was seeing through the eyes of the Spirit. As this woman came up for prayer in each service, the Lord showed me that there was a creature that looked similar to an octopus with several tentacles wrapped around the woman's eyes. Every time I prayed, the anointing of God would hit her and knock off one of the tentacles.

During the second prayer, a second tentacle was supernaturally removed. During the third prayer, a third tentacle came off. Finally, on the last night in the last service, the woman came forward with a single tentacle still wrapped around her eyes. It was like a spirit of blindness, the main demon that had kept her bound in a world of darkness. When I prayed for her the last day, the last tentacle came off and she could see clearly.

The Lord revealed to me that at times, demonic obstructions hold us or cling to us with several arms. Every time you pray under the anointing, *something happens*. You can count on that. The Lord would say to many of us, "Don't get discouraged. Keep praying through until the last tentacle comes off and you see the healing and deliverance!"

ENDNOTE

1. 1 John 1:7.

FOUR

What Is Your Job Description?

I'll never forget the time we were ministering in the bush country of northwest Zambia in Africa, because God used that experience to teach me something about my calling and "job description" in His Kingdom. The Lord healed many people in the crowd of 10,000, but I remember one man who hobbled to the meetings on homemade crutches. His ankles were curled beneath him, and his legs were grotesquely twisted. He had been in that condition for more than 55 years.

After receiving prayer, his legs straightened out and he began to leap up and down with excitement (I have to believe that this scene was very similar to the sight Peter and John saw in Acts 3:3-9). He just couldn't stop jumping for joy! I also prayed for a 16-year-old boy who had been confined to a wheelchair by polio since the age of one. His mother had wheeled him to a place in the prayer line, and after he received prayer, he slid down onto the ground and stayed there as I continued down the prayer line.

Suddenly I heard a clamor in the crowd and saw several severely handicapped people about a hundred yards away from me begin to jump up and down! I just had to go back to take pictures of these miraculous healings, knowing that God alone could do such signs and wonders. While I was walking back to that area, I watched as the boy who had been crippled with polio suddenly jumped to his feet and began to run! By the time I reached the spot where the boy had been lying on the floor, he had already zoomed past me!

The boy's mother was weeping so deeply that her body was shaking with convulsive sobs as she clung to the empty wheelchair where her son had spent so many years of his life without hope. When she saw me approaching, she immediately fell to the ground and began throwing handfuls of dirt over her prostrate body. My interpreter told me she was saying, "Thank you, great chief, for coming to Africa and healing my son." I gently pulled her to her feet and told her, "Dear mother, I want you to know that *I am just a little servant of the Greatest of Chiefs*. His name is Jesus, and He is the One who has healed your son today."

Then another mother cried out to me in a plaintive voice, and I turned around to see a desperately poor woman wearing a tattered skirt and only a scrap of cloth over her shoulders. (The problem here wasn't a lack of propriety or "civilization," but extreme poverty. In such remote regions, few people can afford shoes or other luxuries. Most can only afford one piece of clothing.)

This poor woman said, "Please, sir, I don't care about myself. But can you pray for my little girl?" I looked around and said, "Yes, but where is your little girl?" Then the woman raised her skirt and there, hiding beneath her mother's ragged covering, was a little 3-year-old girl. She was wearing a torn skirt and a dirty blouse, but I could still plainly see the huge boils that covered her body and went deeply into her flesh.

"MAHESH, THIS IS HOW I FEEL…"

I knew the little girl was in terrible pain. To make matters worse, when the mother bent down to show me what was wrong with her little girl, her own shawl fell from her shoulders and I saw that one side of the woman's body had literally been eaten up with a disease that looked like leprosy or a consuming fungus of some kind. I knew this precious mother was in great pain too, but she wanted me to pray for her daughter.

I held them both in my arms, and I prayed for them with all my heart. As I turned away, the mother spoke to me with big tears streaming down her face and said, "Thank you, sir, for coming from America and blessing us poor people."

I couldn't hold back the tears and the compassion I felt in that moment. As I walked away, I felt the Spirit of God ask me, "Do you feel compassion for that woman and her little girl?" I said, "Yes, Sir." Then He said, "*Mahesh, this is how I feel toward all the people in the nations. They are hurting and broken without the message of My Son, Jesus Christ. I want **you** to help them. Share the message of life.*"

WHERE IS THE ARMY?

The Texas Rangers who kept law and order in the Old West left an inspiring legacy. A sheriff in a certain Texas town sent an urgent telegram to Ranger headquarters that said, "Send an army! The town has turned into a mob. They are rioting, and anarchy is threatening to destroy us!"

The sheriff received a characteristically terse reply: "Meet the four o'clock train."

The following afternoon, the anxious sheriff and an even more anxious mayor waited impatiently on the platform as the train pulled in. They watched as a single Texas Ranger calmly stepped onto the platform with his Winchester rifle in hand. The townsmen excitedly looked from the Ranger back toward the train, and when the train finally pulled away, their faces began to lose color again. They met the Ranger and anxiously asked, "Where is the army?"

The Ranger looked them in the eye and said matter-of-factly, "One riot, one Ranger." That's all it would take because that Ranger knew who he was, what he represented, and the full extent of his powers as an officer of the law.

My message to you is simply this: "God's got a riot for you, Ranger." Your job description is to feel what God feels for the world and to *do something about it*. As far as God is concerned, you are the deputy with the authority, the badge, and the weapons of enforcement He left behind to deal with the works of the enemy.

Consult Your Written Job Description

All three synoptic Gospels (the Gospels of Matthew, Mark, and Luke) record the day Jesus gave His disciples the authority and the command to cast out demons and heal the sick:[1]

Then He said to His disciples, "The harvest truly is plentiful, but the laborers are few. Therefore pray the Lord of the harvest to send out laborers into His harvest." And when He had called His twelve disciples to Him, He gave them power over unclean spirits, to cast them out, and to heal all kinds of sickness and all kinds of disease (Matthew 9:37–10:1).

This job description was really a partial one for two reasons. First, it was a faint mirror image of Jesus' own call from Isaiah 61. It was but a foretaste or sample of what would come to pass *after* Jesus had finished His work on the Cross and given His followers the incredible gift of the baptism in the Holy Spirit beginning at Pentecost. Second, the disciples ran into a seemingly insurmountable obstacle later when they encountered the demon that refused to budge below the Mount of Transfiguration (see Matt. 17:21; Mark 9:29). That was the day the disciples learned about the "hidden power" of fasting and prayer in the ministry of deliverance and signs and wonders.

WHY ME, LORD?

Many Christians go out of their way to avoid responsibility for others, but they don't realize that they are simply following the pattern of Cain, who asked the Lord the same question in different terms, "Am I my brother's keeper?" The Lord's answer is still the same: Yes.

Jeremiah the prophet bluntly stressed the eternal consequences of our responsibility to help rescue others when he prophesied, "... *Thus says the Lord: 'Execute judgment in the morning; and deliver him who is plundered out of the hand of the oppressor, lest My fury go forth like fire and burn so that no one can quench it...'"* (Jer. 21:12).

James the apostle warned us in the New Testament, *"Therefore, to him who knows to do good and does not do it, to him it is sin"* (James 4:17). What "good" am I talking about? Let me illustrate this with an incident that occurred in the childhood years of my wife, Bonnie.

When Bonnie was just seven years old, she and her cousins were playing hide and seek in the barn at the Elkin's ranch in New Mexico. Bonnie chose what she thought was a safe hiding place and backed into the darkness between two grain elevators. Dressed only in shorts and a shirt and wearing a pair of rubber thongs on her feet, she crouched in silence, nearly touching the barn wall.

Suddenly, from a spot immediately behind her, Bonnie heard the frightful hiss and rattle of a deadly rattlesnake that was about to strike! In terror, Bonnie bolted and ran to the house to fetch her dad. As they returned to the barn, Bonnie looked down and suddenly realized that she was wearing only one thong.

Bonnie's father entered the barn along with some of the ranch hands and came out a few minutes later carrying a huge, dead rattlesnake. Locked in its fangs was Bonnie's other thong! What a vivid picture of our escape from satan, sin, and death through the death and resurrection of Jesus Christ.

Millions of people are naively crouched in a dark place, playing life's little games in what they believe to be a safe place. But the reality is that there is a ruthless serpent, the devil, who is harboring an aggressive and evil desire to destroy all humanity. On our own, we are totally unprepared, unprotected, and unable to ward off the serpent's attack. But God is calling the world to "run to Daddy" and His hands (the Church) to dispatch the snake. Jesus did it all at Calvary, but He is depending on the Church to spread the news and dispatch the snakes. Unfortunately, many of our own members are also playing life's little games as if the snake were just a dream or a myth. We know the truth, we have the power to set people free, and we have a command and a commission to do just that. Now what?

The last words Jesus spoke to His disciples while He was on the earth offer us even more clues about our job description:

Later He appeared to the eleven as they sat at the table; and He rebuked their unbelief and hardness of heart, because they did not believe those who had seen Him after He had risen. And He said to them, "Go into all the world and preach the gospel to every creature. He who believes and is baptized will be saved; but he who does not believe will be condemned. And these signs will follow those who believe: In My name they will cast out demons; they will speak with new tongues; they will take up serpents; and if they drink anything deadly, it will by no means hurt them; they will lay hands on the sick, and they will recover." So then, after the Lord had spoken to them, He was received up into heaven, and sat down at the right hand of God (Mark 16:14-19).

Evidently the followers of Jesus took Him at His word, because they didn't sit around debating His final statement. According to the final verse in Mark's Gospel, they became *doers* of that word: "*And they **went out and preached everywhere**, the Lord working with them and **confirming the word through the accompanying signs**. Amen*" (Mark 16:20). I have a question: When did this stop? Why? And on whose authority?

Who on earth could possibly have more authority than Jesus Christ? Which one of the apostles could be blamed for teaching that Jesus' final words on the earth could possibly "pass away"? What hint is there in the Gospels that Jesus set forth such a strong statement while knowing all along that it would "pass away" like so many sayings of fallen men? The only answer is obvious—Jesus' words *never pass away*. We are still expected to be in the Gospel-preaching, demon-defeating, disease-healing, prisoner-freeing, oppressed-releasing—and yes, dead-raising— business of Mark 16:14-18! And that can only be done God's way, through lives devoted to prayer and fasting, and to absolute faith in the risen Son of God.

The apostles and disciples of the first century were people who prayed and fasted often. They manifested every single work seen in the earthly life and ministry of Jesus Christ, and this pattern of supernatural ministry and bold outreach continued well into the second century (long after the death of Paul and the original disciples of the Lamb). The ministry declined because the intimate relationship between God and man declined as apathy, heresy, and man-made religious forms and politics crept into the Church.

It is time for us to take back the territory the enemy has stolen from God's people. God wants us to dwell heart-to-heart with Him in intimate relationship and obedience to His will—exactly as Jesus prayed on the day He surrendered Himself to His accusers (see John 17). When we reclaim our inheritance as the sons and daughters of God and begin to seek His face in prayer and fasting, all the miracles of the Gospels and the Book of Acts will come roaring back into the everyday existence of the Church! It is as simple as that.

> *I do not pray for these alone, but also for those who will believe in Me through their word* [you and I]; *that they all may be one, as You, Father, are in Me, and I in You; that they also may be one in Us, that the world may believe that You sent Me. And the glory which You gave Me I have given them, that they may be one just as We are one: I in them, and You in Me; that they may be made perfect in one, and that the world may know that You have sent Me, and have loved them as You have loved Me. Father, I desire that they also whom You gave Me may be with Me where I am, that they may behold My glory which You have given Me; for You loved Me before the foundation of the world. O righteous Father! The world has not known You, but I have known You; and these have known that You sent Me. And I have declared to them Your name, and will declare it, that the love with which You loved Me may be in them, and I in them* (John 17:20-26).

The evidence is overwhelming. The job descriptions Jesus gave to His followers almost 2,000 years ago still apply to His followers today. Just as the disciples were told in Matthew 17:21 that they would have to fast and pray to overcome the most difficult obstacles in life and ministry, so will you and I have to commit to prayer and fasting today. Just as the disciples of old were expected to preach the Gospel, command repentance, pray for the sick, and cast out devils, so the same is expected of you and me! My next statement may rock you, but it is in the Bible. You have been given the authority to raise the dead as well, although this must be done strictly at the command and direction of God. I believe that the Church in this generation will begin to see the dead raised as a sign and wonder on a level never before seen in Church history. I also know it will never happen until God's people discover and practice the hidden power of prayer *and fasting.*

Are you a disciple of the Lord Jesus Christ? Let me clarify that point if there is any confusion: If you are a believer in the Lord Jesus Christ, then *you are a disciple*! What is the job description of a disciple of Christ? Jesus said it best:

> *And these signs will follow those who believe: In My name they will cast out demons; they will speak with new tongues; they will take up serpents; and if they drink anything deadly, it will by no means hurt them; they will lay hands on the sick, and they will recover* (Mark 16:17-18).

The people Jesus commissioned and sent out two-by-two were ordinary folks like you and me, but it didn't matter to the Son of God. Their job description included the responsibility to heal the sick, raise the dead, and cast out demons. Jesus said, *"Freely you have received, freely give"* (Matt. 10:8b).

The Church has walked away from this job description in favor of a rewritten version that seems to prefer hiding behind four walls while sitting in a pew, limiting God's light to a select chosen few. No, God's Word and purposes haven't changed. God has called us to be healed, and to carry His healing mantle with us wherever we go. It costs us a price to carry that level of anointing and healing in our lives; it will take a life of disciplined prayer and fasting. My friend, if we are not "aiming" for any particular target or goal in Christ, then we will surely succeed at hitting nothing. Paul would have nothing to do with this "do nothing, know nothing, risk nothing" approach to the Christian life. He boldly declared:

> *Brethren, I do not count myself to have apprehended; but one thing I do, forgetting those things which are behind and **reaching forward** to those things which are ahead, **I press toward the goal for the prize of the upward call** of God in Christ Jesus. Therefore **let us, as many as are mature, have this mind;** and if in anything you think otherwise, God will reveal even this to you* (Philippians 3:13-15).

You will meet people in need that I will never meet. It happens every day in your daily routine of going to work, going to the grocery store a half mile from your house, or filling the gas tank in your car. Jesus did it with the disciples, and God is doing it with you: "One riot, one Ranger." One supernatural need, one Spirit-filled believer anointed with the *power* of God and the authority to use it!

A LESSON FROM HISTORY

History is a great teacher, and those generations that have heeded its lessons have been wiser than those that did not. The difficult period surrounding World War II and the Jewish Holocaust holds many examples that demonstrate the urgent need for servants of the light to stand up and be counted in the war against the servants of darkness.

During the dark years of that war, certain individuals arose whose courage and vision served as a standard of light against the ominous death cloud that settled over Europe. Despite the almost total oppression and tyranny experienced under the onslaught of Hitler's Third Reich, a few dared to exercise their freedom to choose the righteous path; and in so doing, they provided life for others.

Oskar Schindler was a businessman and a Nazi who intended to build a financial and social kingdom for himself by exploiting the occasion of war. Schindler was not a successful businessman before or after the war, but during that dark season of Hitler's reign of terror, Oskar Schindler came to be involved in the rescue of 1,200 Jewish people whose lives and family lineage would otherwise have been extinguished forever in the ovens of Nazi Germany's extermination camps.

Somehow this businessman had a change of heart. His entire value system was transformed, and as a result, he began to turn his munitions factory business into a life-saving business. One by one, Oskar arranged to have Jewish refugees and prisoners transferred to his factories as "slave labor," and he purposely ordered his workers to turn out flawed munitions. As the times became more and more desperate, Schindler began to sell off his personal assets and often risked his own life to "buy" the lives of more and more Jewish people before they were shipped off to the death camps of the Nazi SS corps. Finally, as Allied forces began to enter Germany's borders and liberate Europe, Schindler—still officially considered a member of the Nazi party—was forced to flee Germany.

A motion picture depicting his true story flashes the scene of Schindler's final good-bye to the hundreds of Jewish refugees he had personally rescued from Hitler's ovens. As he looks at the people, Schindler realizes just how few there are in light of the many he saw hauled away to their deaths. As he looks at his few remaining possessions—his wedding band, and the very car he needs to escape arrest and possible death—Schindler cries out:

"Ten more lives, ten more could have been saved! *I could have done more, I could have done more!"*

As I watched this dramatic scene in the movie, *Schindler's List,* my heart leapt in my chest. I thought, *Had more people who were not forced to wear the yellow star of the Jew exercised the freedom they had to choose righteousness—more people would have lived!* Oskar Schindler spent the entire fortune he made to buy lives from Hitler's death lists. The 1,200 lives he saved have since multiplied to more than 6,000 lives, yet 6 million Jewish lives were brutally snuffed out, and with them millions more who would have been born.

There is a prophetic voice crying out through Oskar Schindler's words that says with the authority of God, "Without Christ, every soul will perish. The ultimate purpose for all believers is to rescue those held under sin's bondage of death. The one commission for everyone who believes on Jesus is *to save others."* The only eternal aspect of our lives on earth is our investment in the eternal life of others.

What is your job description? To be like Jesus in word and deed. To do His works and more by His command! The best way to close out this chapter and prepare our hearts for the next is to recall and meditate on the ancient prophecy that defined the call of our Messiah and defines your call to this generation as well:

The Spirit of the Lord is upon Me, because He has anointed Me to preach the gospel to the poor; He has sent Me to heal the brokenhearted, to proclaim liberty to the captives and recovery of sight to the blind, to set at liberty those who are oppressed; To proclaim the acceptable year of the Lord (Luke 4:18-19).

You too are called and anointed by the Spirit of the Lord to preach the Gospel of hope to the poor. You also have been sent and empowered to heal the brokenhearted and to proclaim liberty to the captives. As a disciple of Jesus, you have been given divine authority in His name to open the eyes of the blind and to set at liberty those who are oppressed of the devil. And today as perhaps never before, you are anointed to proclaim the "acceptable year of the Lord"!

Now for the most difficult question. Are you prepared to do the works of Jesus as you have been commanded to do? Then you must be prepared to pay the price and say with Jesus to your generation, *"Today this Scripture is fulfilled in your hearing"* (Luke 4:21b). The first step to success and triumph for all of us may be the hardest, as we find the place of true humility.

ENDNOTE

1. See also Mark 6:7-13; Luke 9:1-6.

━━━━━━━━━━━━━━━

Chapter FIVE

Humility: The Position of Triumph

During a 40-day fast, the Lord visited me and told me that a worldwide revival was coming and that it would bring an unprecedented harvest of souls and glory to the earth. I believe that we have entered the post-Charismatic era or wave of anointing. We are beginning to see the first droplets of that rain of anointing and glory, the first tokens of that great harvest the Lord described to me some years back.

There are signs and seasons in the natural that point to this coming rain. As Charismatic and Pentecostal churches around the world anticipated the centennial anniversary of the Azusa Street outpouring, record rains yielded a once-in-a-lifetime bloom in Death Valley, California. Desert seeds that had lain dormant for 100 years suddenly sprang to life after the unusual rains in this extreme desert climate of Western America. Experts began to call this phenomenon the "hundred-year bloom," and people streamed from all over the world to see this amazing sight.

A century after one of the most influential outpourings since Pentecost, thousands of expectant believers flocked to Los Angeles, California, for the Azusa Street Centennial Celebration. I was asked to be a representative of the healing anointing along with Dr. Oral Roberts and Kenneth Copeland during this worldwide celebration. The final day of the event was held at the Los Angeles Memorial Coliseum. Hours before the opening ceremony, crowds wrapped around the perimeter of the stadium! The atmosphere was charged with the spirit of unity and expectation. Speakers, leaders, and over 45,000 believers gathered together for a once-in-a-lifetime experience. As I stepped to the podium to speak, the healing presence and thick glory of God filled the stadium. The crowd hung on to every word, ready for a touch as I shared the story of the resurrection of a 6-year-old African boy, Katshinyi, and my own son's miraculous deliverance from death. As I announced that "Jesus is the same yesterday, today and forever. Stretch forth your hand to heal…in the name of Your holy servant Jesus," the arena filled with a roar of praise and expectation as an impartation of the Holy Spirit fell.

The rains of the Holy Spirit are coming upon His last day church as never before! I believe that God is releasing the power again like He did at Azusa Street. A fresh Pentecost is coming, a hundred-year bloom! Yet the Church can only begin to operate in the power of the Spirit when its members obtain the grace of God in their lives. How do we obtain grace? *We humble ourselves.* Proverbs 3:34 tells us that God "*…gives grace to the humble.*"

Jesus, our ultimate model of ministry, discipleship, and leadership, showed us the way. The apostle Paul told the believers at Philippi:

Let this mind be in you which was also in Christ Jesus, who, being in the form of God, did not consider it robbery to be equal with God, but made Himself of no reputation, taking the form of a bondservant, and coming in the likeness of men. And being found in appearance as a man, He humbled Himself and became obedient to the point of death, even the death of the cross. Therefore God also has highly exalted Him and given Him the name which is above every name (Philippians 2:5-9).

There is much confusion about the words *humble* and *humility* because they bring up images of outwardly humble actions performed by people who are anything but humble on the inside. Most of these outward efforts have the same effect as someone who says, "I thank God that I'm not proud anymore." Even the saying of such a thing instantly puts us back in the domain of pride! Even the outward actions that many suppose are the fruit of humility can place us in jeopardy again by creating pride in our works. Yet there is a biblical path to humility.

Whenever people come to me and say, "Brother Mahesh, pray for me so I can be humble before God and stay that way," I tell them about David and the Psalms. In the context of praying for those who were his enemies, David wrote, "*...I humbled myself with fasting...*" (Ps. 35:13). The Hebrew word translated as "myself" in the New King James Bible is *nephesh*, which can be literally translated as "my *breathing creature.*"[1] The King James version translates this word as "soul." In Psalm 69, a classic Messianic psalm of the Lamb, David wrote prophetically:

*Let not those who wait for You, O Lord God of hosts, be ashamed because of me; let not those who seek You be confounded because of me, O God of Israel. Because for Your sake I have borne reproach; shame has covered my face. I have become a stranger to my brothers, and an alien to my mother's children; Because zeal for Your house has eaten me up, and the reproaches of those who reproach You have fallen on me. **When I wept and chastened my soul with fasting**, that became my reproach* (Psalm 69:6-10).

The scriptural way to humble yourself before God is by fasting. There are times when you need to tell your soul or your "breathing creature" who is boss. We need to discipline our souls, and one of the ways we do that is by fasting. When we humble ourselves before God, we receive His grace and power. The apostle Peter wrote:

Likewise you younger people, submit yourselves to your elders. Yes, all of you be submissive to one another, and be clothed with humility, for "God resists the proud, but gives grace to the humble." Therefore humble yourselves under the mighty hand of God, that He may exalt you in due time (1 Peter 5:5-6).

If we can live in this atmosphere of genuine humility and not get impatient, then in due time God will exalt us. The problem in the United States and in many Western nations is that our performance- and pleasure-driven culture produces some of the world's most impatient people. We have been carefully taught to expect instant gratification through decades of skilled advertising, marketing, and entertainment propaganda in the media.

If you doubt my claim, then sit in front of your television with a stopwatch for just one evening. You will quickly notice that in almost every situation comedy or drama program, the central character can solve the problems of life in only 30 minutes or an hour! (And most of the problems arise because they can't get what they want, the way they want it, as fast as they want it.) The advertisements that interrupt only serve to reinforce this message, enticing us to believe that if we just buy this product, we can instantly live a better life. We have been conditioned to expect a quick fix that requires little personal sacrifice or perseverance. Well, life doesn't work that way. God says if we remain humble, then He will exalt us.

HE CHOSE THIS FATHERLESS HINDU BOY

Consider God's promise again. He says that *He* will exalt us. That is a tremendous promise from One who never lies or fails to keep His promises. I have been so humbled by the Lord's inexplicable grace and mercy to me. He led me through several years of prayer and fasting, and then He chose this fatherless Hindu boy who was raised in a poor family in a remote place in Africa to conduct miracle services for people from 86 nations! He even used me to minister miracles in Jerusalem, only a few yards from the very streets where Jesus walked!

As mentioned previously, every week we are reaching a flock of over 800 million households with the Gospel of Jesus through our television program, *The Watch*. We regularly receive testimony from people who have received salvation, healing and deliverance through this program. The Arab world is receiving the Gospel in their native language, and our outreach is stretching across to India and Africa. Western nations bound in secular humanism are being touched by the supernatural power of miracles, signs and wonders.

Who am I? Why have Bonnie and I been blessed with the privilege of seeing God work so many awesome miracles in our ministry? It surely isn't because of us—it is all God's doing. I can only say, "Lord, Your mercy is so wonderful toward this little fatherless boy. Thank You, Jesus!"

You can *choose* to live a life of continual humility before God. Constantly pray to the Lord Jesus, "Lord, I want to remain humble. I choose to humble myself before You, and I don't want You to be forced to humiliate me!" It is fun to let the Lord exalt and anoint you for His work. But you must never grasp for it. Humble yourself, and the Lord will lift you up.

One of the greatest of all Scriptures on the subject of humility, fasting, and prayer is found in the timeless passage in the Book of Second Chronicles:

> *If My people who are called by My name will **humble themselves**, and **pray and seek My face**, and **turn from their wicked ways**, then I will hear from heaven, and will forgive their sin and heal their land* (2 Chronicles 7:14).

When the Bible says "humble themselves," it doesn't mean you should just wear "bad" clothing and say, "I'm so humble." It is referring to the scriptural way of humbling yourself *through fasting* described by King David in the Psalms.

God wants us to *humble* ourselves individually and corporately, through fasting according to Psalm 69; to *pray*; to *seek His face* and to turn from our wicked ways, or *repent*. For His part, He promises that He will *hear* us, He will *forgive* our sins, and He will *heal* our land.

AMBASSADORS OF DELIVERANCE

Part of our God-given commission as ambassadors of the Gospel and of reconciliation is our impartation of grace and anointing to cast out evil spirits. As ambassadors of the King, wherever we are, that part of the commission goes with us. God's Word says, "*A wicked messenger falls into trouble, **but a faithful ambassador brings health**" (Prov. 13:17). I feel that the Body of Christ is moving to a new level or place of corporate authority to cast out evil spirits from individuals, and also from neighborhoods, houses, and entire communities. Evil spirits are real, and their commission is to torment humanity. Our commission is to take up our cross daily and follow Jesus. Jesus came to *break every yoke*.

Many forms of demonic oppression and influence will yield to the anointing of the word of command spoken by Spirit-filled believers. However, there are certain demonic obstacles or strongholds that won't break until you combine prayer with fasting and tap into the *power* of the Spirit as Jesus did.

This extreme resistance to spiritual authority is commonly seen in cases of chronic drunkenness, alcoholism, drug addiction, homosexuality, witchcraft and occult involvement, spirits of suicide and depression, and rebellion or lawlessness. I've often seen this kind of stronghold associated with the curse of poverty. When an individual or family is struggling under this kind of demonizing influence, they will find that no matter how much money they earn, their finances always seem to dwindle away through an unbroken string of accidents, car repairs, bouts of joblessness, or other calamities. That is an outward indication that a curse of poverty is at work.

MANY CHRISTIANS FEEL ALMOST HELPLESS

Another area often resistant to the normal prayers of believers is the area of disease. Some diseases, such as cancer, the HIV/AIDS virus, Ebola Hemorrhagic Fever, SARS and Avian Bird Flu, along with almost all forms of mental illness, carry such a paralyzing weight of fear and invincibility with them that many Christians feel almost helpless in their efforts to overcome them through prayer. I understand their feelings and frustration, but we also know from the Scriptures that even these deadly diseases and demonic strongholds *must* bow their knee to the authority of the risen Lord.

In Milwaukee, Wisconsin, a Hispanic gentleman brought his child to me who was suffering from epileptic seizures every two to three minutes (it was strikingly similar to the situation Jesus dealt with in the Gospels). When I first saw the boy during the service that night, I thought he was trying to disrupt the meeting, but he wasn't. He was having seizures. When this father brought his boy to the front for prayer, I knew it was one of those impossible situations that wouldn't yield unless the glory of God came on the scene.

When I prayed over the child, I had to rely totally upon God because I really didn't know what would happen. I had been fasting and praying, and when I took authority over that demon, the foulest smell you can imagine filled the entire meeting room in that hotel! When that evil spirit left the boy, we could all smell the odor of burning sulfur and rotten eggs, but we didn't care because the boy was instantly healed! I found out that this boy had suffered from an almost constant series of epileptic seizures day and night since his birth. I don't know how he sustained himself or how his brain had not been destroyed due to the violence of the seizures. All I know is that somehow God protected the boy until the day the evil spirit was cast out.

WHEN I HAD NO STRENGTH, GOD RAISED THE DEAD!

God exploded the anointing for mass evangelistic outreaches in my life in 1985, in what was one of the darkest moments of life for Bonnie and me. While pregnant with our son, Aaron, Bonnie developed complications that put her and our baby at risk of death. She was confined to bed for three months until Aaron was suddenly born four months early!

Everything that could possibly go wrong *went wrong*. Day after day, we battled for the life in Bonnie's weakened womb. In the midst of this intense battle against anxiety and darkness, God broke through and told us, "Laugh! You need to laugh." What seemed so inappropriate at the time turned out to be "just what the doctor ordered." A friend handed us some Bill Cosby tapes, and we listened to his hilarious antics every day for weeks and laughed until we ached. God was right. That hour spent in laughter made us feel like we were getting a breath of air after swimming underwater for a long time.

At just 25 weeks in her pregnancy, Bonnie delivered a very premature baby boy. We named him Aaron, and he was dying. He only weighed one pound three ounces. He had a severe brain hemorrhage, total lung malformation and gangrene in his intestines. The doctors said he would live for perhaps a few hours, maybe a few days, but if he lived, he would be in a vegetative condition. Our little Aaron barely hung onto life.

In the very middle of that life-and-death struggle with the illnesses and complications of his birth, I was scheduled to travel to Zambia and Zaire in Africa to conduct healing meetings and training sessions with Brother Derek Prince and an apostolic team. Bonnie insisted at that time that I keep the commitment in Africa. I feared that Bonnie would have to bury our son alone while I was gone. Leaving her and my son was one of the hardest decisions of my life. Before I left, I remember anointing my tiny son with oil and telling Aaron, "Daddy loves you, and I probably won't see you again, but I give you to Jesus."

Brother Derek and I had some great meetings and outreaches in the northwest province of Zambia to train about 2,300 young pastors and evangelists. Suddenly, in one of the meetings, the Spirit of God came upon Derek, and he started crying. He had been talking about apostolic teams and the importance of discipling people, but then he said to the people there, "I taught everything I know to Brother Mahesh. God is going to teach him some *more*, and the fruit in his life will produce ten times the results that mine have."

I started weeping and so did he, and then I thought to myself, "*How can that ever be? I cannot touch anywhere near the intellect and the anointing and amazing teaching ability that Derek Prince has.*"

I went on alone from Zambia to conduct an evangelistic outreach in Kinshasa, Zaire. On the very first night of the outreach, God brought in 100,000 people, and by the end of the week nearly 360,000 people were attending the meetings. (The Zairian army was on hand to help control the crowds, and they documented the official count in each service.) Brother Derek later told me that the biggest crowd he saw in his Zimbabwe meetings amounted to one-tenth or 36,000 people, and the Lord spoke to me and said, "*See, I can do anything.*" I sure knew it wasn't me.

The power of the Holy Spirit was there to heal. It was during that outreach in Zaire, in the atmosphere of glory, that the Lord gave me a very unsettling and very specific word of knowledge during one of the meetings. I was still carrying the heartbreaking burden of my concern for Bonnie and little Aaron who was clinging to life half a world away, and *that was the time* God decided to say to me as clear as a bell, "There is a man here *whose son died this morning*. Call him up. This day *I am going to resurrect his son!*"

I did what the Lord told me to do and announced to that massive crowd in front of me that God said there was a man there whose son had died that morning. A murmur that turned to a roar swept through the people, and then the interpreter told the people the rest of God's message, that if that man would come to the front, then He would raise the boy from the dead. I'll never forget the sight of that man running up to the front. Nor will I forget how I felt in that moment, for I knew there was no way that I could raise that boy from the dead. Only God could restore life and breath to that man's son.

I tell the complete story of God's miraculous power in this situation in my book, *Only Love Can Make a Miracle*,[2] but I will tell you this: Katshinyi had died at 4 o'clock in the morning of cerebral malaria. By 12 noon, the 6-year-old body of Katshinyi sneezed twice and rose up. God had miraculously raised him from the dead! (A copy of Katshinyi's death certificate is reproduced in my autobiography.) All the glory for this miracle goes to God alone, of course. The wonder and faithfulness of the Holy Spirit is so awesome. At that same hour, the anointing to heal went to my son's dying body in Florida. Today Aaron is a healthy, strong young man who is brilliant and totally committed to the Lord. In my weakness, God revealed His strength. I give much credit for it to the lifestyle of prayer and fasting the Lord graced me to embrace. I think those times helped "move me out of the way" so God could reveal His glory without hindrance from my flesh. The Lord laid a foundation and was then able to cleanse me in such a way that I could hear more clearly what He was saying and cooperate with Him. And coincidentally, I had just completed a 40-day fast prior to this trip.

The key to defeating dark strongholds is twofold. First we must tap the *power* of the Spirit through the combination of prayer and fasting; and second, we will overcome in the largest battles in this generation only when we pray and fast *together* and unleash the incredible power of the Body of Christ on its knees. The Lord has commissioned me to help train up an army of men and women who will do the *works* of Jesus. An unavoidable part of the works of Jesus begins with *prayer and fasting* because these were the *first works of Jesus* in His mission to destroy the works of the enemy.

THE DIFFERENCE BETWEEN VICTORY AND TRIUMPH

When God's people are attuned to the heart of God, He will warn and equip us long before a device or attack of the enemy surfaces to threaten us. Long before the 9-11 terrorist attack exposed the danger of enemy cells operating within U.S. cities, one of our watchmen at The Watch of the Lord™ headquarters had a dream about a dark intruder trying to get inside Charlotte's "city walls." She felt perhaps the intruder was in fact already in and planning harm. The watch leaders felt this revelation was a prompting from the Lord, and we began to pray. The Holy Spirit focused our prayers to specifically come against a terrorist cell of radical Jihadists working in Charlotte. We asked for light to shine on the full operation and for a joint task force of natural authorities to move in and take the cell down.

One of our watchmen, a federal agent, was working on just such a case involving a terrorist cell, but the information was top secret and known to none of us but him at the time. Because he was involved in the investigation, he was not able to speak about the case in any manner. Yet he heard us praying the very strategies and specifics needed to successfully complete the operation. The next week a joint task force of over 200 policemen, FBI agents, and members of three other federal agencies conducted a sting operation and uncovered and stopped an extensive illegal interstate operation using our city as a base to raise funds for support of terror in the Middle East. The arrests went off without a hitch! All the persons indicted as a result of the operation were convicted of the crimes charged, and the cell was shut down.

Fasting sharpens the focus of our prayers and our accuracy in discerning what to do. Look closely at the Bible narrative of the triumph of King Jehoshaphat and Judah in the Book of Second Chronicles when two major enemies and other forces came in overwhelming numbers to conquer Judah:

> And **Jehoshaphat feared, and set himself to seek the Lord, and proclaimed a fast throughout all Judah. So Judah gathered together to ask help from the Lord; and from all the cities of Judah they came to seek the Lord.** Then Jehoshaphat stood in the assembly of Judah and Jerusalem, in the house of the Lord, before the new court, and said: "O Lord God of our fathers, **are You not God in heaven, and do You not rule over all the kingdoms of the nations,** and in Your hand is there not power and might, so that no one is able to withstand You? Are You not our God, who drove out the inhabitants of this land before Your people Israel, and gave it to the descendants of Abraham Your friend forever?
>
> ...And now, here are the people of Ammon, Moab, and Mount Seir; whom You would not let Israel invade when they came out of the land of Egypt, but they turned from them and did not destroy them; here they are, rewarding us by coming to throw us out of Your possession which You have given us to inherit. O our God, will You not judge them? For **we have no power** against this great multitude that is coming against us; **nor do we know what to do, but our eyes are upon You.**" Now all Judah, with their little ones, their wives, and their children, stood before the Lord. Then the Spirit of the Lord came upon Jahaziel the

son of Zechariah.…And he said, "Listen, all you of Judah and you inhabitants of Jerusalem, and you, King Jehoshaphat! Thus says the Lord to you: **'Do not be afraid nor dismayed** *because of this great multitude,* **for the battle is not yours, but God's.**

…You will not need to fight in this battle. Position yourselves, stand still and see the salvation of the Lord, who is with you, O Judah and Jerusalem!' Do not fear or be dismayed; tomorrow go out against them, for the Lord is with you." And Jehoshaphat bowed his head with his face to the ground, and all Judah and the inhabitants of Jerusalem bowed before the Lord, worshiping the Lord. Then the Levites of the children of the Kohathites and of the children of the Korahites stood up to praise the Lord God of Israel with voices loud and high. So they rose early in the morning and went out into the Wilderness of Tekoa; and as they went out, Jehoshaphat stood and said, "Hear me, O Judah and you inhabitants of Jerusalem: **Believe in the Lord your God, and you shall be established; believe His prophets, and you shall prosper."** *And when he had consulted with the people, he appointed those who should sing to the Lord, and who should praise the beauty of holiness, as they went out before the army and were saying: "Praise the Lord, for His mercy endures forever." Now when they began to sing and to praise, the Lord set ambushes against the people of Ammon, Moab, and Mount Seir, who had come against Judah; and they were defeated. For the people of Ammon and Moab stood up against the inhabitants of Mount Seir to utterly kill and destroy them. And when they*

had made an end of the inhabitants of Seir, they helped to destroy one another. So when Judah came to a place overlooking the wilderness, they looked toward the multitude; and there were their dead bodies, fallen on the earth. No one had escaped.

When Jehoshaphat and his people came to take away their spoil, they found among them an abundance of valuables on the dead bodies, and precious jewelry, which they stripped off for themselves, more than they could carry away; and they were three days gathering the spoil because there was so much (2 Chronicles 20:3-7,10-15,17-25).

POSITION YOURSELVES FOR MORE

The word of the prophet to Judah and to the Church today is this: *Position yourselves.* There is a place *beyond victory* called *triumph.* Victory is being able to defeat your enemies. But triumph goes far beyond mere victory. When you triumph, you come out of the battle with *more than you had before!* God wants to give you *more.*

First we need to learn how to stand together in times of trouble and crisis. Unfortunately I have noticed a sad fact: People who are going through painful situations find more sympathy out in the world than in the Body of Christ! I think it is because we have trained ourselves to act more like sharks than believers when we see someone who is wounded, bleeding, and floundering in the waters of adversity or failure. The members of the Body of Christ seem more determined to attack and cut up their wounded members than to rush to their side with support, healing, and gentle correction if needed.

The Lord will not tolerate this in the Bride of Christ. We are to support each other in grace and mercy because we are yoked together and united in Christ. If one falters, we all falter. That is why the fasting family of God wants to see every individual family in its body blessed. If one is affected, we are all affected, so it behooves us to stick together and say, "Lord, we seek Your face."

There is an exponential release of power when we corporately harmonize our prayer and fasting for victory. A few years ago, a precious family that had moved from Chile to be a part of our church experienced the victory that comes with this kind of corporate fasting. Their son, Michael, had just turned eight years old when his teachers reported noticing strange head movements during class. His parents began to observe him, and it quickly became evident that there was a problem and that it was getting worse. Michael's head jerked around as he watched television, his tongue flicked in and out, he blinked constantly, he would unconsciously point his middle finger at people, and he would grunt repeatedly, even in his sleep. The progression of the symptoms was alarming.

Michael was diagnosed with Tourette's syndrome, a very serious nerve disorder. For the next four years he and his family struggled with this disease. Their Harvard-trained neurologist was able to control the condition with strong medication, but soon the medication caused such severe side affects that Michael had difficulty even breathing. A gauntlet of other medications was just as unsuccessful in halting the progression and severity of his tics. By the end of the third year he had almost one tic per second. During this time, we prayed for Michael, and our local church body surrounded his family with love, offering support and practical assistance. But the problem persisted, and his family was emotionally and physically worn down.

In the fall, Michael was supposed to enter into sixth grade. The frequency of his tics had made it almost impossible for him to function in the classroom. His parents were contemplating pulling him out of school when I asked if we could put him at the top of our prayer list during a corporate 21-day fast. For three weeks our church fasted and asked God to intervene for Michael. Some people fasted the entire time. Others took turns for shorter periods. Soon after the end of the fast, Michael's parents noticed that he had not had any tics at the breakfast table. The last time they had counted his tics at a family meal, he had had 54 tics per minute. Now he seemed to have nothing. For days they kept looking for signs of the disorder, but there was never another tic. There had been no change in medication, no special treatment, nothing but the fast. God had healed Michael. Michael has been completely well for several years now. He is a strong student, an excellent artist, an active soccer and basketball player, and a regular volunteer at our home church. We attribute his healing completely to the Lord Jesus Christ and to power of a corporate fasting.

THE SECRET PLACE OF TRIUMPH

What was the first thing King Jehoshaphat did when the crisis arrived? He called a fast so the entire nation could bow before the Lord's face and pray, "Lord, we humble ourselves." When we take a low position, we open the door for God to take the high position. I was participating in a corporate fast one time when someone heard about the fast and ran up to me and said, "What are you fasting for?" I confess that I was irritated by the way she asked the question. Her unspoken statement was that our attitude in the fast was one of "getting something" from God. "Give me this, and give me that and that." That was not our attitude, nor should it be.

When we humble ourselves before God, our first desire must be *for Him*. We should humble ourselves to seek His face, not merely His hand. "We want *You*, Lord. Above all, we want You. We want Your glory and Your presence."

Moses knew the secret to blessing. When the Lord gave him an opportunity to go out and be successful and promised to send an angel along with him, Moses said, "No way. We are not going one step farther unless You go with us."[3]

The Lord was waiting for Moses to ask Him that! Because the Lord said, "I have My bags packed already, just waiting for you to ask!" The Lord is waiting for you to ask Him to get involved in your situation. The quickest and surest way to do this is to *humble* yourself and then to *position* yourself for triumph, not just victory, according to God's pattern in Second Chronicles 20:12.

EZRA FASTED AND PETITIONED GOD

The prophet Ezra also faced an agonizing situation that put a large number of families at risk. Artaxerxes, the king of Persia, gave Ezra gifts of gold, silver, and other goods for the restoration of the Temple at Jerusalem. Then Ezra had to lead a group of Levite families and other devout Jewish families—and the rich treasure of gold and silver—through very dangerous territory without any armed escort. With every step that they walked away from the center of Artaxerxes' power center in Babylon, the Jews walked deeper into danger and lawless territory. Many of the inhabitants along the way had been openly hostile to the Jews in the past. Ezra the priest did something of critical importance before he began the dangerous journey from Babylon to Jerusalem:

> *Then I **proclaimed a fast** there at the river of Ahava, **that we might humble ourselves before our God**, to seek from **Him the right way** for us and our little ones and all our possessions. For I was ashamed to request of the king an escort of soldiers and horsemen to help us against the enemy on the road, because we had spoken to the king, saying, **"The hand of our God is upon all those for good who seek Him**, but His power and His wrath are against all those who forsake Him"* (Ezra 8:21-22).

Ezra spoke by faith when he told King Artaxerxes, "God is strong enough to defend us." But he did more than talk—he knew there was spiritual warfare involved. You don't just say things about God; you back it up with prayer, with fasting, and with intercession. This is what the body of believers called the Church has been called to do. We are to become living prayer and living intercession before God. And we are daring to say with Ezra, "God will stand for us."

> *So we fasted and entreated our God for this, and He answered our prayer* (Ezra 8:23).

FOLLOW THE PATH TO REPENTANCE AND TRIUMPH

All of us have habits or thought patterns that we need to deal with. We have weaknesses and sins that seem to defeat us on a regular basis, and to make matters worse, we know that it is impossible to "pretend" before God and get away with it.

Some of us fight depression; others constantly battle evil tempers and fits of rage. Nearly every parent I've ever talked with has admitted there have been times when they grew angry with their children unfairly. They always "kick themselves" later and say, "Why did I do that?" We need to echo the prayers of King Jehoshaphat in Second Chronicles and say to the Lord, "Before this enemy I have no might. I humble myself; give me victory." This releases the Lord to cleanse us internally, to give us a "spiritual colonic" and cleanse us inside as we humble ourselves. Our constant prayer must be, "Lord, where there is iniquity, shine Your light upon us that we can fellowship with You."

ENDNOTES

1. James Strong, *Strong's Exhaustive Concordance of the Bible* (Peabody, MA: Hendrickson Publishers, n.d.), soul (#H5315, H5314).

2. Mahesh Chavda with John Blattner, *Only Love Can Make a Miracle* (Ann Arbor, MI: Vine Books/Servant Publications, 1990).

3. See Exodus 33:1-17.

—⊷———————⊷—

Two Causes of Casualties in the Ministry

My lovely wife, Bonnie, stood up to greet the people attending a revival conference and began by saying that she didn't have anything really profound to say. Then she said some very profound things that relate directly to why so many called-out and anointed ministers of God have fallen by the wayside recently and why so many feel overwhelmed today—even though God is moving across the world in this moment on a scale we have never seen before! This is what Bonnie said:

"I hope that you are like I am—I am *so desperate for the living God* in this hour. The thing that I have found is that there are two kinds of people. There are people who are living completely absorbed in the stress and the harried nature of our time; and there are people who are seeing that scene from a distance and crying out, 'My God, I don't want to be a part of that.'

"I hope that you are in that group of people who are saying, 'Lord, *there is more to existence than what I see in this world!*' I just want to encourage you: God is coming in this hour with power that we have not seen. I truly believe that we are beginning to live in a time that is likened to the time when Abraham sent his servant to find a bride for his son, Isaac. God is pouring out His Spirit in a fresh way.

"One thing I want to say to you is this: *Just get desperate for God. Get desperate* and *stay desperate*. And the more He touches you, the more that should make you hungry. And the more He fills you, the more that should make you thirsty. And the more He pours out His Spirit on you, the dryer you ought to realize you really are! Because God is awesome, awesome, awesome.

"Another thing I want to encourage you in is this: We have become very lazy in this culture about gathering with the people of God and listening to the Word of God. Let me just exhort you and plead with you to be like Bartimaeus when he threw off his beggar's robe. There is a robe of apathy and arrogance that lays on us that is expressed with excuses like, 'I'm OK, God. I can sit at home on Sunday morning, maybe go to church once every month or not at all, maybe get what I need from TV.'

"Folks, we need to get in the living presence of the living God, with His living Body. I just want to exhort you and plead with you: 'Don't weary in well-doing. Don't get tired of going to church—*get hungry*.' And the more you go to church and the more you feel like you're not getting anything out of it, the more you ought to be coming! Because you're hungry and you need to be in His presence.

"Enjoy the presence of the Lord and reach out to Him like blind Bartimaeus. Put down every robe, everything that would hinder you or keep you sitting in that dark, blind, or beggarly place. And allow your hunger to cry out, 'Son of David, have mercy on me!'"

God's grace is free, but it's not inexpensive. It costs us to embrace it fully! Jesus was filled with the Spirit, but it cost Him something to return in the power of the Spirit. Many of us are satisfied with the first level of the anointing, but we need to always be hungering for more. The Holy Spirit desires to lead us into the wilderness to teach us how to follow Him, breaking and molding us into vessels that can carry the anointing with power. Fasting releases new levels of the anointing into our life and ministry. It is a discipline that tests, trains and equips us to walk in power and authority, strengthening and transforming our inner self to carry greater levels of His glory.

I want to focus on two causes of "casualties" in the ministry. These problems aren't new or exotic, but they show up again and again, and they account for some of the greatest failures and missteps in the Bible and in the history of the Church. I believe that many of the casualties we see in the ministry are caused when people who have received the fullness of the Spirit *are released into public ministry without the power of the Spirit*. Just being full of the Spirit is not enough. We all need a time of seasoning when the Lord teaches us and perfects us before we go out to help others. If you go out "half-baked" in the things of God, then you can become a casualty and a sad statistic of the poorly prepared. Jesus dealt with the first problem immediately after He cured the demonized boy whose affliction defied the delegated anointing of the disciples:

*And when they had come to the multitude, a man came to Him, kneeling down to Him and saying, "Lord, have mercy on my son, for he is an epileptic and suffers severely; for he often falls into the fire and often into the water. **So I brought him to Your disciples, but they could not cure him.**" Then Jesus answered and said, "**O faithless and perverse generation,** how long shall I be with you? How long shall I bear with you? Bring him here to Me." And Jesus rebuked the demon, and it came out of him; and the child was cured from that very hour. Then the disciples came to Jesus privately and said, "**Why could we not cast it out?**" So Jesus said to them, "**Because of your unbelief;** for assuredly, I say to you, if you have faith as a mustard seed, you will say to this mountain, 'Move from here to there,' and it will move; and nothing will be impossible for you. However, **this kind does not go out except by prayer and fasting**"* (Matthew 17:14-21).

We noted earlier that Jesus had commissioned these men. He had given them authority to heal the sick, to cast out demons, and even to raise the dead; then He said, "Go." Yet they had run into a solid wall of evil that just wouldn't move for them. This hindrance and obstacle prevented the disciples from bringing deliverance and freedom to this family. Was the authority Jesus had given them still there? Yes. Jesus had given them the legal authority to cast out devils, but for some reason they had run into a new type of demonic force that just wouldn't yield to the level of anointing they had in their lives.

As a result, their public failure to defeat this demon had brought reproach on everything the disciples stood for. I imagine that more than one of the remaining nine disciples left at "the bottom of the hill" that day were beginning to wonder if they were really cut out for the job Jesus gave them. They probably began to wonder, "Did Jesus *really* say 'cast out demons...'?" Once the demon was cast out and Jesus and His disciples were in a private place, He pointed out *two things* that were problematical in the disciples' lives and ministry:

1. *The disciples failed because of unbelief.*

2. *The disciples failed because there are certain demonic strongholds that will not yield to secondhand authority.*

The solution for both is found in the final comment Jesus made about the situation with the spirit of epilepsy afflicting the young man at the foot of the mountain. This comment came *after* the Lord's classic teaching on the power of "faith as a mustard seed." And by the nature of His statement, He was talking about demonic power that wouldn't yield even to this "faith as a mustard seed." Immediately after His comments about mountain-moving faith, Jesus said:

> *However, this kind does not go out **except by prayer and fasting*** (Matthew 17:21).

Certain victories will not be achieved in our lives or in the lives of others unless we *combine* our prayer with *fasting*. We have heard a lot about prayer in recent years, and there are a lot of books about prayer lining the shelves of Christian bookstores around the world. Unfortunately, there has been very little *living proclamation* or *personal impartation* on the subject of fasting. In other words, very few people have *done it* and borne fruit from it before writing a book on the subject.

Fasting is like a hidden truth that has been forgotten or purposely misplaced and ignored by the Body of Christ over the last century. Yet I have found that fasting is one of the greatest weapons that God has given to His end-time army! God's destiny is for us to see our families set free. He wants entire generations and nations to come to salvation. He wants to see our local churches immersed in genuine revival. He longs to see our cities enjoying salvation and redemption in a wonderful way. He wants to bring His supernatural power to heal and deliver the lost and to spark revival again, not only to cities but to entire nations! But there are two major problems blocking the way to this kind of supernatural visitation in the Church and the world.

UNBELIEF IN THE CHURCH

One of the major sins of the Church has been the sin of unbelief. Beginning with the Patristic fathers, the church has been shaped by the idea, "Seeing is believing." Rather than pressing in for the truths given to us in the Bible, much of the church has embraced a theology that explains away the lack of power in the church as a sign that the authority, miracles, and deliverance promised to us are not for today. Doubt and unbelief are the opposite of faith. God's Word warns us that "without faith, it is absolutely impossible to please God," but you would never know we believed it judging from our actions.[1] I really believe that the Lord raised up various "faith" teachers years ago to counter a serious slide into skepticism and anemic, faithless religion in mainstream Christianity. Many congregations in North America had adopted a "form of godliness" while denying the *power* thereof.[2] Many aspects of the so-called "faith movement" were very good and healthy for the anemic Church, but side-by-side with the good came gross excesses in motives and deeds for which many need to repent. The truth is that we need to receive the truth of having faith because we are called to be a people of faith.

We need faith mixed with our works because ultimately, everything in this world and in the world to come is measured by *fruit*. What have we done to back up our talk of following Jesus and doing His works? Where have we disobeyed, and where have we obeyed God in our lives and ministry? Where is the good fruit from our tree? What kind of water is flowing from our fountains?

Frankly, I am a bit embarrassed to draw this comparison because we come up so short as a people, but even a casual glance at the history of communism on this planet reveals that this ideology made astounding progress and growth in a matter of only a few decades! Communist expansion marched on for 70 years until its followers had engulfed almost one third of the world under their rule! The same antichrist spirit is threatening our world today through the violent rise of Jihadist terrorism and the cancerous effects of secular humanism.

Meanwhile much of the Church has lumbered (or slumbered) along for 2,000 years while supposedly directing all its resources into the fulfillment of the great commission personally delivered into its care by Jesus Christ. We have had a measure of success (if you use a small scale), but nowhere close to the success we should have had. Most of the progress in spreading the Gospel came from the work of the first-century Church, and from key individuals who experienced life-changing visitations from God through *prayer and fasting* such as Martin Luther, the Moravian brethren, John Wesley, George Whitefield, D.L. Moody, and others. I think God is waiting to see what happens when we stop waiting for "just a faithful few" to do the work. He wants to see His *Church* rise up as a whole, complete Body in all its resplendent glory as His spotless Bride. It is time to stand in the face of the enemy in the power of Christ's Kingdom manifest in miracles, signs and wonders. Fasting is a key to release this power. The world will never be the same!

The reality is that the Church has seemingly been powerless to bring the family of man into victory and freedom, *even though we have been given the name and authority of the Son of God for our use.* Does this sound familiar? It sounds to me like we have revisited the crowd scene at the bottom of the Mount of Transfiguration again! *We suffer from the same problems that plagued the disciples of Jesus in the first century.*

I'm happy to say that Jesus isn't limited to what He sees today. Because He holds time in His hand, He also sees what shall be *tomorrow.* He gave the Church a promise concerning the last great sign of His coming in the Gospel of Matthew:

> *And this gospel of the kingdom will be preached in all the world as a witness to all the nations, and then the end will come* (Matthew 24:14).

Embedded within this prophetic promise is the cure for what ails us. It contains a prophetic command, a perfect Model, and the fulfillment of a promise. We are commanded to proclaim "this Gospel." God didn't give us a multiple-choice command or a smorgasbord assignment plan. We are anointed to proclaim "this Gospel" and "this Gospel" only. It is the same blessed Gospel that Jesus proclaimed. It is the same Gospel the apostles proclaimed, the Gospel for which they willingly laid down their lives. It is the same Gospel that disciples like Stephen and Philip of Samaria proclaimed. *This Gospel,* accompanied by signs and wonders confirming the Word.

GOD FOCUSED ME ON JESUS

Our primary model in the proclaiming of that Gospel is Jesus Christ. Is there any other leader you would rather follow than Jesus? This isn't just a rhetorical question that you don't have to answer. If you really believe that Jesus Christ is Lord and Savior, and that He is the only begotten Son of God, then you should *model your life and ministry after Jesus Christ* more than any other. If you dare to do this, then God will dare to fulfill another promise from Jesus that we have examined: *"Most assuredly, I say to you, he who believes in Me, the works that I do he will do also; and greater works than these he will do, because I go to My Father"* (John 14:12).

"This Gospel," which was proclaimed by Jesus and the disciples, was always accompanied by mighty signs and wonders, miracles and healings. These things also began to happen in my ministry after God focused me on Jesus and His divine pattern of combining prayer with fasting. This is more important than ever in our day because of the great humanist clouds of doubt and unbelief that have covered the Western nations. The Church is called and anointed to break through those clouds and to proclaim *this Gospel* to all the nations with signs and wonders confirming the Word.

PROPHETIC PREVIEW OF THE GOSPEL AND THE WORLD

One reason that the Lord is moving so strongly upon His Church is because any great harvest produces a great need for great "storage and processing" capacity. Several years ago the Lord told me, "I am preparing you for *China*," and I felt strongly that He would bring down the "Bamboo Curtain" of mainland China in our generation. Within a matter of just a few years, I had conducted multiple mass evangelistic outreaches in the island nation of the Republic of China (Taiwan). We had some of the largest crowds in their history, and no matter what size of facility we rented for the meetings, we had to turn away hundreds each night! I was later told that some of the miracles seen during those landmark meetings had never before been seen in the Republic of China. Now the population of the Republic of China is only a fraction of the entire Chinese population, most of whom live on mainland China, which is communist-ruled as of this writing.

Those meetings were very difficult to conduct because of the spiritual opposition we encountered there. They were some of the first "power" evangelistic outreaches ever conducted in Taiwan, and I knew I was battling demon gods and goddesses that had been worshiped from generation to generation in that 3,000-year-old culture. How did I do battle with such an imposing array of dark powers that said, "Hey, we possess this land! Who are you?" I came proclaiming the Gospel.

At times I felt like I was engaged in intense hand-to-hand combat, but God gave us a wonderful harvest anyway. Hundreds and hundreds of Chinese people came forward each night to repent of their sins and dark allegiances and be saved. Yet despite all those early successes, the Lord told me, "You haven't seen *anything* yet!" Just think about it: What happens when you inject the life-changing power of "this Gospel" into a basically unevangelized nation of *1.4 billion people*? (This is "a thousand million people" plus four hundred million more for good measure.)

There is a thriving underground house-church movement in Communist China today; but I discovered when I went there that it numbers "only" in the millions. This is nothing when compared to "a thousand million" people. "Well, what about communism?" Communism has been successful in accomplishing only one thing: It created an intense spiritual vacuum. In the words of Joseph, *"But as for you, you meant evil against me; but God meant it for good, in order to bring it about as it is this day, to save many people alive"* (Gen. 50:20).

The Church is called to fill every vacuum created by totalitarian governments and godless philosophies with the Gospel proclamation confirmed with signs, wonders, and miracles.

There is no way you and I can fulfill our divine call without the *power* of God. When we find ourselves ministering in a place where the whole atmosphere is impregnated with demon powers, we need more than delegated authority; we need to walk in a demonstration of power in the anointing that comes through fasting. When you have to blast the door open to break down satan's gates, then you need the *power* of God demonstrated in signs and wonders to follow your preaching of the *Word* of God. This has been God's preferred method of evangelism since the Day of Pentecost nearly 2,000 years ago, and it has resurfaced in every major revival, renewal, and awakening to come since then.

Now I have to tell you something by the Spirit of God: *The Lord is preparing you* to actively participate in this great harvest!

Yes, He is preparing *you*. Your local church is also preordained to be *actively involved* in this end-time revival and Gospel proclamation. Yet you still have the power to say yes or no to Him.

When the curtain of communism finally falls and the borders of China open to the proclaimed Gospel, our assignment will be to *immediately* train up *one million pastors* to train and pastor at least as many new churches in that great country! Now do you understand why God is so clearly putting together end-time apostolic ministries on a global scale? He has no patience with our squabbles over whether or not apostles, prophets, and miracles still exist—He wants these people *released* to do their job, and He wants them *now*. He wants you to step into your supernatural calling too, but it all comes with a price.

Another way in which first-century evangelism differs greatly from our "modern" methods is that no one functioned alone. God is aggressively creating the same kind of networks through divine relationships that helped the early Christians spread the Gospel around the known world in one generation. I know that through God's grace I can do certain things well. He has given me the kind of ministry that can "kick the door open" into certain cities and nations through supernatural signs and wonders, but that is only one of the anointings God has ordained for mass evangelistic campaigns. My assignment is to win the lost and plant churches in the thousands, but there is absolutely no way that I can personally pastor those churches or disciple the hundreds of thousands of new believers in those churches. That brings up the next question that the Holy Spirit is asking believers around the globe: *What is your assignment? Are you willing to pay the price?*

BACK TO BASE ONE

Let me return to the theme of the Lord in this book: One of the things God is doing to prepare us to participate in the end-time revival is this: He is transforming us into men and women who will pay the price by learning how to *pray and fast.* We must begin to use this great weapon of the harvest. That is why *there is no substitute for prayer and fasting* if we really want to bring the victory of Christ into the lives of our families, our churches, and our nation! Jesus said it, not me. He said, *"However, this kind* [of demonic bondage, oppression, obstruction, and hellish control] *does not go out except by prayer and fasting"* (Matt. 17:21; see also Mark 9:29).

It is likely that at some point in your life and ministry, you have been stopped cold or greatly hindered by obstructions. That thing, whatever it is—be it a demon power, unforgiveness, or a clinging sin that keeps cropping up again and again—will not budge until you combine your prayers with fasting. I've learned through practical application and experience that it is like throwing a nuclear weapon into your spiritual arsenal. Imagine that you've been using hand grenades of prayer to move a massive mountain of unbelief, hindrances, or demonic obstructions in your life and ministry. When you combine your prayers with fasting, you suddenly drop a hydrogen bomb on the mountain that is blocking your call and divine assignment. I'm not talking about a "slight" difference. Fasting boosts the intensity and effectiveness of your prayer at least tenfold, and often a hundredfold! This is why the hidden power of fasting has become such an imperative from the Lord. It's a crucial end-time tool for proclaiming the Gospel to the nations with signs and wonders confirming the Word we preach.

In the same way that I faced a life-and-death struggle for souls in the Republic of China or in Africa, so the Church in North America is locked in "hand-to-hand" combat here for our nation. We are in a battle against secular humanism and the relentless efforts of the godless to remove all vestiges of God from our nation and its history. The Church *must* wake up and use the weapons God has given us to reclaim the inheritance that God has destined for America. *This* is no time to sit back and watch God's parade go by. The Church needs to hunger for and welcome the fresh Pentecost that God wants to pour out on us. In a sense, the Church is God's "corporate Esther," who was birthed and brought to maturity "for such a time as this."[3] His sovereign Word to us is this: "Revival is at hand. Forget your past hurts and wounds, and catch the vision for your calling in God!"

You are called to be a part of this revival, and the first way you can participate is through prayer and fasting. Start interceding for the lost today. Go on a fast once a week and intercede for your nation, praying, "Lord, *give us revival.*" My vision is to see at least one million believers joined together in a continuous fast, praying before the risen King for the harvest of souls. What would happen if each of us would commit to pray and fast at least one day per month for our nation, the Church, and our families!

The Lord wants us to be released in the *power* of the Spirit, but that can come only as we continually say yes to the wooing of God's Spirit—even when it makes us feel very uncomfortable (as it often does). It is through this process that God removes doubt and unbelief from our hearts through the cleansing flow of His convicting Spirit and healing presence. There are simply no shortcuts to His presence, and the surest path to holiness, purity, and power is found in the powerhouse combination of prayer with fasting.

I was in the middle of a 40-day fast while ministering in Washington, D.C. at the House of Representatives. The Lord visited me nightly during my seven-day stay in Washington. What I did not realize was that God was simultaneously visiting Bonnie at our home in Florida. We had both received a prophecy for the local church where we were serving at the time along with Brother Derek Prince. When I compared notes with Bonnie, we discovered that the core message of the two prophecies matched word for word! The Lord told both of us that He wanted the local church body to pray and fast for 21 days. I received an additional word that we were to gather together as a body from 5 A.M. until 7 A.M. every day, and the Lord said, "If you do not do this, *I will depart* and you will not even notice that I have gone."

I had already witnessed many situations in which the Lord's presence had left a congregation, but the people were still "going through the exercises," although their life was gone. We were on the verge of that as a congregation. All the elders agreed that Bonnie had a true prophetic word along with my added word from the Lord about the early morning gathering. We subsequently called the church body to a 21-day fast[4] and asked that as many people as possible meet together for corporate prayer each morning from 5 to 7 A.M.

I had an out-of-town ministry commitment and so did Derek Prince; yet, even though the two of us had to leave, the church was supposed to start the fast on the following Monday. On the first day of the fast, a total of *five people* out of a 600-member congregation showed up for the corporate gathering. On the next day, only *two people* showed up. One of the two people there that morning was a man with a strong prophetic gifting—he always traveled with me when I ministered in Africa. This man began to weep that morning when the Spirit of God came on him. He spoke to the church during the regular Wednesday night service the next day, and said, "The Lord told me, '*I am here, where are My people?*'"

I flew back home that same night, but I didn't find out until about midnight what had happened. After this man spoke to the people, the Spirit of the Lord began to fall upon the children first. Then He descended on a number of adults as well. I knew something unusual was afoot when my little 4-year-old daughter, Serah, came into my bedroom at about 4 o'clock in the morning and shook my shoulder. She said, "Daddy, wake up! It's time to go to church." Now little Serah loved her sleep, but here she was at my bedside fully awake, and ready to go to church. We found out that many of the parents in the church congregation were being wakened by their children.

Bonnie told me that the day before I got home, she had been awakened by a loud knock on the door—*at 4 A.M.* When she got up and answered the door, nobody was there. She gathered up our children and went to the church building, and when she opened the door, the glory of the Lord was so strong that she fell on the floor right there! When God's glory came down, all the children had simultaneous visions. Whenever the Lord walked in, we would all know He was there, and everyone could see the same thing. One hundred and fifty people turned up, then 200 people turned out. We were engulfed in a spirit of revival, and it was an awesome thing to behold. People started repenting of sins—men who were thought to be examples of holiness began to weep uncontrollably and repent of their compulsive involvement in pornography and addiction.

One of the most remarkable characteristics of this visitation was our sense of the literal presence of God hovering over us when the Lord walked into those meetings. All I could do was just weep in a kind of "holy terror" because He was there in such breathtaking holiness and glory. I didn't even want to lift up my head because I could so strongly sense the holiness of God in that place. God's presence stayed with us week after week, and we were in true revival—even as early as 1986! Derek Prince shared that in his 40 years of ministry at that time, he had never experienced this level of God's anointing or tangible presence. It was one of the most glorious experiences we had ever experienced corporately.

If this was so powerful, then why didn't the church world hear about it like it heard about God's visitation in Toronto, Ontario, and Pensacola, Florida? The answer is that *we did not know how to steward the presence of God*. The Holy Spirit didn't ask us "how to come" to us. He sovereignly chose to reveal Himself as the Spirit of repentance, and He called us as a people to *repent*. Unfortunately, we did not understand that *repentance is a word of blessing*. The only reason we are able to genuinely repent before God is because the Holy Spirit gives us the grace to repent.

Week after week, the Spirit of God would descend on us in His heavy, weighty glory and lead us to our knees in continual repentance. Meanwhile, some of the leaders began to feel uncomfortable about it all. They were (and are) good brothers who dearly love God, but they began to feel so uncomfortable with the way the Holy Spirit kept "hovering" over us that they wanted to "move on." The problem was that the Spirit of God didn't want to "move" anywhere. They said, "That's enough repentance. Let's go into joy," so in the end we left the Holy Spirit behind to party when God wanted to complete a deeper work of repentance in us and perhaps in the nation as a whole.

We often think God should be satisfied with our repentance or obedience in a particular area, when His focus isn't on us at all! Sometimes He is satisfied with our repentance on "Day 1," and He wants to work repentance in our families, churches, cities, or nation in "Days 2 through 21." But then we get impatient. We want to have a celebration party before there's anything to celebrate about! We left God's place of grace so we could "move into joy," but as we left Him behind, very slowly the hovering presence of the Spirit began to fade away too, along with His anointing.

All of us who witnessed that remarkable visitation were profoundly affected by it for years to come. I can still recall the wonderful presence of God that came down in those meetings, and I learned that we not only need to learn how to "bring down the glory," but we should also learn how to "steward the glory" with honor, respect, and obedience so He will *stay* with us.

God gave John the Baptist one "yardstick" to pick out the Messiah from the crowd of humanity. He said, "*Upon whom you see **the Spirit descending, and remaining** on Him, this is He who baptizes with the Holy Spirit*" (John 1:33b). During the Charismatic movement, we learned how to honor God and see the Holy Spirit *descend* upon us in a concentrated way from time to time, but we didn't know how to encourage His presence to remain among us.

I believe that a lifestyle of disciplined fasting and prayer (individually and corporately) is one of the elements required of a people who enjoy the *abiding* or lingering presence and glory of God. We need to learn this lesson because, believe me, when you get touched by the glory of God, there is nothing on earth to compare with it! I believe I would do anything, I would walk a thousand miles on my knees to be around the glory of God. The key to overcoming the two great causes of casualties in the ministry is the intimacy borne out of hunger and personal surrender through prayer and fasting.

ENDNOTES

1. See Hebrews 11:6.

2. See 2 Timothy 3:5.

3. See Esther 4:14.

4. The Lord did not necessarily expect each person to observe 21 days of continuous fasting, although some had the grace to do so. The church members were to take turns fasting as the Lord gave them grace so that throughout the 21-day fast, one or more believers were ministering in God's presence in an unbroken chain of 24-hour prayer, fasting, praise, and worship.

Chapter Seven

Arrows of Pain, Arrows of Triumph

There is a cost that comes with the call and the anointing of God. When we finally acknowledge that our lives are not our own and that we have been bought with a price, then everything changes. We begin to feel the urgency of God moving us inexorably to our particular part of the harvest fields.

I remember the driving urgency I felt when ministering to hundreds of thousands of people in Central Africa where the HIV and AIDS viruses have infected more than 1 in 4 adults and an untold number of children! In some cities in the region, more than 7 out of every 10 pregnant mothers tested positive for either HIV or AIDS and were very likely to pass the fatal disease to their unborn babies during gestation, birth, or breast-feeding.[1] Many of those people were dying, and the Spirit impressed on me the urgency of delivering the Gospel of life to them before their lives ended. At the time of this writing, HIV/AIDS is the leading cause of death in Africa, with 6,500 Africans dying every day.[2]

When the passion of God flows so strongly to the lost and hurting, His servants must sometimes make difficult decisions and take arrows to the heart to obey their Lord. This has happened to many of God's servants over the centuries; it happened to me while I was conducting five evangelistic outreaches in the island nation of Taiwan, the Republic of China.

I was told by Christian leaders in Taiwan that if the regular churches in that nation saw two people come to the Lord in a year, there was great celebration. We were seeing hundreds come to the Lord every night during those meetings! Although the spiritual battle in the heavenlies was one of the most intense I had ever witnessed in my life, we were still seeing the harvest being gathered in miraculous ways.

Right in the middle of all this glorious victory and demonstration of God's power, I received a devastating phone call. My older brother was seriously ill. He had never married, but had literally sacrificed his own career and life to take care of my mother and to raise me and my little sister after my father died. He had poured himself into us.

I had prayed for my brother two and a half years earlier after he became seriously ill the first time, and God had miraculously sustained him and raised him up. This time he was near death in London, England, and all I could do was communicate by telephone from the other side of the world. I wanted so badly to take him in my arms and tell him that I loved him. I wanted to say, "Thank you for taking care of me so faithfully." All I could do was press on. The outreaches I was conducting had been advertised for one and a half years. Hundreds of people were flying in from Singapore and Hong Kong. Thousands of Chinese people were being saved in the process—people who had never heard the Gospel with power. Then I received word that my brother had died.

CONFLICT OF DUTY

In the tradition I come from, when a member of the family dies, every living male must attend the funeral—especially the oldest remaining son. I phoned my mother in London from the Republic of China and she said, "Honey, I've never asked you for anything in my life. You come and be with your brother."

Had I gone to London for the funeral, I would have had to cancel a minimum of five nights: two nights to make the trip from Taiwan to London, one night in London, and two nights to return to Taiwan. Meanwhile, hundreds of lost souls were being saved *each night*. My mother was asking me to come and honor the one man who gave up everything for me, and it was a legitimate request for a very important reason. Yet, if I did so, hundreds and perhaps thousands of souls would most likely be lost forever. (You see, the Lord is bringing us to the point where we have to make difficult choices that challenge some of the most treasured priorities in our lives.)

I had to call my mother and say, "Mother, I love you, but I have to answer the Lord's call." I stayed in China and did not go to my precious brother's funeral. I can't begin to tell you how much it hurt me to make that call and to preach despite my pain. But the glory of God came down in a new measure that night and in every meeting afterward, and we saw hundreds of Chinese people get saved each night. I know I will see each of them in Heaven, but I had to make a hard choice that night in Taiwan.

God is taking all of us through journeys that will be hard at times, that will force us to make some difficult choices revolving around the question, "Whom do you love more?" The indescribable pain I felt as I made that choice lingered and remained with me for some time. I deeply love and respect my mother, and there are no words to describe the love, gratitude, and respect I have for my brother. Yet I had to answer God's call and deliver light to those in darkness.

ONE WORD FROM JESUS

The pain of that decision troubled me until the Lord came to me with a word that gloriously healed me. *All it takes is one word from the Lord to drive away every tear and every hurt in your heart.* Do you know what He told me? He said, "Mahesh, you were doing My work. Because you couldn't go, *I went.*" If He went, then you know what that means! He just took my brother by the hand and said, "Let's go." I had led my brother to the Lord several years earlier, so I knew he was saved. But Jesus Himself went to personally take my brother into the presence of the Father!

The Bible pictures us as soldiers and warriors in God's army. As a soldier under God's command, you may encounter certain things in your personal life that conflict with God's call on your life. If you give those things to God and obey His call, then He will personally take care of the things you give up to obey His command.

As the Lord of lords and King of kings described by John in the Book of Revelation, Jesus is the same yesterday, *today*, and forever.[3] He is ready to avenge His people Israel and His Church with the sword of His mouth and to lead us to total and instant victory, but we must first learn the two prerequisites of victory in every battle:

1. We must cast away all sin and uncleanness in our lives through His blood.

2. We must obey every command and follow each strategy the Lord gives us without deviation or hesitation through fear.

If you were to go through history books and various forms of the media, you could come up with quite a list of problems, plagues, and hindrances that face us in this generation. I know your list would include such demonic strongholds as abortion, rampant drug use, and the seducing New Age doctrines and pervasive humanism tainting the minds and institutions of virtually every Western nation on the planet. These things are demonic in origin and are wreaking havoc among humankind and even the Church.

The answer to these evil influences is found in Christ and His Church. No matter how many principalities and powers of spiritual wickedness threaten to destroy righteousness in this nation and take our cities captive, God has an answer. Jesus revealed that answer in His high priestly prayer in the Gospel of John. It is God's glory revealed in us.

Jesus has passed along to us the same commission that empowered and guided His early mission to redeem us. His call is our call, only He has already finished the work of the Cross. Now it is our job to take the good news to the world. Are we willing to observe the ultimate fast of God described by the prophet Isaiah? God is commissioning us as His end-time army with this ancient declaration of war:

> *The Spirit of the Lord God is upon Me, because the Lord has anointed Me to preach good tidings to the poor; He has sent Me to heal the brokenhearted, to proclaim liberty to the captives, and the opening of the prison to those who are bound; To proclaim the acceptable year of the Lord, and the day of vengeance of our God; to comfort all who mourn, To console those who mourn in Zion, to give them beauty for ashes, the oil of joy for mourning, the garment of praise for the spirit of heaviness; that they may be called trees of righteousness, the planting of the Lord, that He may be glorified." And they shall rebuild the old ruins, they shall raise up the former desolations, and they shall repair the ruined cities, the desolations of many generations. Strangers shall stand and feed your flocks, and the sons of the foreigner shall be your plowmen and your vinedressers. But you shall be named the priests of the Lord, they shall call you the servants of our God. You shall eat the riches of the Gentiles, and in their glory you shall boast* (Isaiah 61:1-6).

REBUILDING THE ANCIENT RUINS

This level of divine call demands a supernatural change in our values, direction, and life focus. If a person's values are still carnal, then you know he has not been touched by the glory of

God. John the revelator had a life-changing experience with God; the things he saw in his vision of Heaven are still affecting us today!

Something happens to people when they encounter the living God. I call it "a glorious addiction." Once John saw the glory of God, he was addicted. Once Moses saw the glory of God, he was addicted. Once Paul saw the glory of God, he was addicted. Each of these men brought a part of the glory, government, and power of God in Heaven back to earth with them. Once you taste the heavenly, nothing on earth can even come close to satisfying your hunger and thirst for it.

I believe that in a way it's almost easier to come to Jesus as a total heathen and experience His glory than to grow up in the Church and seek to taste His glory. Too often people who have spent years in an average local church begin to take the glory for granted. Again and again, Christians respond to reports of God's glory descending in meetings with the casual reply, "Oh, I *know* about that. I've heard about it all my life." I tell them, "No, you don't understand. You are talking about 'hearing about' or 'knowing about' a historical figure or event. You *don't know Him* and have not tasted the wonder of His glory!"

That is the problem. I was a Hindu when God suddenly appeared to me in an open vision of Heaven. He shocked my mind and soul, and transported me in an instant from total darkness into total light when I saw a vision of Jesus, whose brightness was greater than 10,000 suns. When I finally awoke the next morning, I was completely captivated by Jesus!

When I first came to America and began attending a fundamental Bible college and church, the people just couldn't understand why I was such a fanatic about Jesus. They said, "You'll calm down. It'll go away." They gave me a little grace because I was just a heathen who had recently been saved (if they hadn't, they would have kicked me out sooner than they did). But as time went by, I began to die inside. Apathy, doubt, and unbelief began to drain away my life. I was stranded in a place where the spirit of religion denied the power thereof.

At first I almost felt ashamed because I didn't have a long heritage in the Church. I soon found out that I wasn't missing anything if the lives and faith of most "historical" Christians were any measure. I have great regard for true spiritual heritage in families that have really passed along a personal, sold-out relationship with Jesus. But most Christians "inherit" only a form of religion that seems determined to deny the *power* of Christ and His glory. Now *that* is not an inheritance to cherish; it is a disease that needs a cure.

God gives us an instruction in Ephesians 6:10 that this end-time army needs to heed:

Finally, my brethren, **be strong in the Lord** *and in the* **power of His might***. Put on the whole armor of God, that you may be able to stand against the wiles of the devil. For we do not wrestle against flesh and blood, but against principalities, against powers, against the rulers of the darkness of this age, against spiritual hosts of wickedness in the heavenly places. Therefore take up the whole armor of God, that you may be able to withstand in the evil day, and having* *done all, to stand. Stand therefore, having girded your waist with truth, having put on the breastplate of righteousness, and having shod your feet with the preparation of the gospel of peace; above all, taking the shield of faith with which you will be able to quench all the fiery darts of the wicked one. And take the helmet of salvation, and the sword of the Spirit, which is the word of God; praying always with all prayer and supplication in the Spirit, being watchful to this end with all perseverance and supplication for all the saints* (Ephesians 6:10-18).

It will cost you if you want to *know God* and see His glory. Like Paul, you will have to lay down all your knowledge and become like a little child before Him. You will have to sign your own death certificate on the cross of obedience and in daily surrender of your life, your agenda, and your priorities in prayer and fasting. Then, as you trust Him to strip your "filthy rags of manmade righteousness and religious credentials," God will give you His own righteousness and "new credentials" that have everything to do with His presence and nothing to do with the approval and pleasure of men.

During the span when the Lord called me to observe regular 40-day fasts, I was sometimes touched by God's glory. In those moments when I was conscious, I no longer wanted to live. I actually wanted to die so I could be with Him. In one moment, His glory transformed my values and perception of life. Yes, I have faith to believe God for a new Mercedes or a house, but I would rather focus my faith and energies on seeing 100,000 people come to Jesus in *one night*!

Material blessings and provisions are nice, but my heart has been transformed by God's glory. I pine for Him, I long for His presence, and I've grown to love and desire the things my Master loves and desires. When we are touched by God's glory, the things of the earth instantly grow dim in comparison. The closer we draw to Him, the more we die. The more we die, the more like Him we become. This is what Paul meant when he said, *"As we behold Him, we are changed from glory to glory."*[4] If you are not in the Spirit, then you cannot see the things of God and experience His glory. If you will pay the price to seek His face in prayer with fasting, then you will experience a life transformation as you literally put on *the strength of the Lord* and *the power* of His might! Now that is the *only* way to fight the good fight of faith.

DON'T PULL BACK DURING CONFLICT

At the time of the Gulf War, Christian and world leaders alike saw many examples of what happens when kingdoms are in conflict. During the final days of battle, the world's leaders argued whether or not Saddam Hussein's military machine should be annihilated or just pushed out of Kuwait. Some said we should treat Hussein as we would any sovereign once he was in his own territory, and their counsel was followed. The combined forces of the Desert Storm task force pulled back, but almost immediately, when it became apparent that Hussein had lied about his vast arsenal of nuclear and biological weapons, America's leaders regretted the decision to withdraw just before toppling Baghdad.

Now, ten years later, our military is fighting in Iraq again because they didn't stay just one more day. General H. Norman

Schwarzkopf, commander of the Allied forces in Desert Storm, said his forces needed one more day to enter Iraq's capital city of Baghdad and topple Hussein's evil empire. Instead, he was ordered to pull back. Now the situation is repeating itself. Opposition and violence in the struggle to create a free Iraq has caused many to say that it is time to "get out." They are satisfied with a partial defeat of the enemy and are unwilling to make the sacrifices necessary to insure the complete victory. The events in Iraq mirror the attitude of many Christians toward spiritual battle. Once the immediate crisis is over, or when the opposition seems too great, we pull back rather than persevering to the end. God wants to give us victory, but He also wants to develop the skill and strength that comes from learning to persevere in the battle. We see this clearly in the events that took place almost 2,800 years ago.

> *Elisha had become sick with the illness of which he would die. Then Joash the king of Israel came down to him, and wept over his face, and said, "O my father, my father, the chariots of Israel and their horsemen!" And Elisha said to him, "Take a bow and some arrows." So he took himself a bow and some arrows. Then he said to the king of Israel, "Put your hand on the bow." So he put his hand on it, and Elisha put his hands on the king's hands. And he said, "Open the east window"; and he opened it. Then Elisha said, "Shoot"; and he shot. And he said, "**The arrow of the Lord's deliverance** and the arrow of deliverance from Syria; **for you must strike the Syrians at Aphek till you have destroyed them.**" Then he said, "Take the arrows"; so he took them. And he said to the king of Israel, "**Strike the***

*ground"; so he struck three times, and stopped. And the man of God was angry with him, and said, "**You should have struck five or six times; then you would have struck Syria till you had destroyed it!** But now you will strike Syria only three times"* (2 Kings 13:14-19).

God assured the victory through the word of His servant, but it is clear that He expected a response from the king: faith and perseverance in battle. If you want to know how to achieve victory in the realm of the Spirit, learn the lesson of Joash and never stop until total victory is yours in Christ. Our God has given us some powerful "arrows" or components of victory, and we need to strike the earth with them until total victory is ours. Developing a lifestyle of prayer and fasting gives opportunity for the Holy Spirit to forge this determination and faith into our spirit.

EIGHT ARROWS OF GOD'S VICTORY

1. Be full of the Holy Spirit (*But you shall receive power when the Holy Spirit has come upon you; and you shall be witnesses to Me in Jerusalem, and in all Judea and Samaria, and to the end of the earth.* Acts 1:8.)

2. Choose your battle. Then seek God for His direction on how to enter aggressive spiritual warfare (*So David inquired of the Lord, saying, "Shall I go up against the Philistines? Will You deliver them into my hand?" And the Lord said to David, "Go up, for I will doubtless deliver the Philistines into your hand."* 2 Sam. 5:19.)

3. Survey the cost and commit to complete victory (*Or what king, going to make war against another king, does not sit down first*

and consider whether he is able with ten thousand to meet him who comes against him with twenty thousand? Or else, while the other is still a great way off, he sends a delegation and asks conditions of peace. So likewise, whoever of you does not forsake all that he has cannot be My disciple. Luke 14:31-33.)

4. Be sober minded. Neither momentary defeats nor successes should cause you to let down your guard and turn back (*Therefore take up the whole armor of God, that you may be able to withstand in the evil day, and having done all, to stand.* Eph. 6:13.)

5. Focus on winning the battle. Do not allow discouragement or distractions to dissipate your commitment to win (*Therefore, my beloved brethren, be steadfast, immovable, always abounding in the work of the Lord, knowing that your labor is not in vain in the Lord.* 1 Cor. 15:58.)

6. Do not let unforeseen obstacles force you to turn back (*But Jesus said to him, "No one, having put his hand to the plow, and looking back, is fit for the kingdom of God."* Luke 9:62.)

7. Be thankful. Once the battle is won, thank God and praise Him for the victory (*But thanks be to God, who gives us the victory through our Lord Jesus Christ.* 1 Cor. 15:57.)

8. Be vigilant. Guard the victory until "the region is stable" (*Be sober, be vigilant; because your adversary the devil walks about like a roaring lion, seeking whom he may devour.* 1 Pet. 5:8.)

These eight "arrows" can serve as our quiver of power for victory. In the Kingdom of God, we must understand clearly that our enemy the devil is roaming around like a roaring lion seeking whom he may devour.[5] Our objectives must always remain clear and uncompromising. Then our faith and God's resources will always supply the strength we need.

I am reminded again of the dark years of World War II when great armies rallied for the causes of good and evil and clashed in both the Western and Eastern hemispheres for the domination of the globe. In the midst of global conflict, we saw great men rise up to lead. Some were infused with incarnate evil as they purposed the demonic goal of annihilating the Jews and imposing their dark dominion on every nation within their grasp. Other men of nobler purpose were placed by *divine plan* in harm's way. Their very birth in that generation demanded their response in body, soul, and spirit, to resist the rise of evil in that day. As Christians, the fact that we find ourselves occupying this age demands our full attention and obedience to the purposes of God in our day as well.

Throughout that conflict, American General George Patton's tenacity and devotion to victory inspired and facilitated some of the greatest Allied victories against Adolph Hitler's Third Reich. General Patton was known to be ruthless when in pursuit of his objective. When the moment came to engage the enemy, Patton would make sure that he and his men *were in the breach*— even though their own supply lines were often falling far behind the rapidly advancing front line of their motorized armored columns.

General Patton gave a great call to courage as he addressed his troops before they engaged the enemy, knowing full well that many of them would be called upon to give the supreme sacrifice by losing their lives or limbs in exchange for the liberation of others. This is a paraphrase of General Patton's speech:

"Men, one day when your grandbaby climbs into your lap and looks up at you and asks, 'Granddaddy, what did you do in the great war?' You will not have to hang your head in shame and say, 'I was shoveling manure in Louisiana.' You will be able to look him in the eye and say, 'Honey, I was right in the midst of the battle when the nations of the world were hanging in the balance!'"[6]

In our day, God is preparing His Church and gathering up His "eagles" for war. He is massing His troops in the face of a wave of satanic outpouring. Even as He foretold through the prophets of old, His own great outpouring of the Holy Spirit upon all flesh is about to flood the earth with His glory, and it will wash away all evil before it.

God's great army is being prepared to "take the prey" by pulling down the strongholds of supernatural evil resistance that are holding humanity in the bondage of terror, sin, and disease worldwide. We must develop perseverance, tenacity, and prevailing patience if we are to wage successful warfare. Above all, we must not pull back, cut back, or turn back until we have totally destroyed the works of the enemy. We have been given a promise of victory, but God is waiting for us to *strike through* until we possess our enemy's gates.

Finally, we need to pay close attention to the admonition of God's Word concerning our confidence in times of conflict, difficulty, and hard decisions:

Therefore do not cast away your confidence, which has great reward. For you have need of endurance, so that after you have done the will of God, you may receive the prom-ise: "For yet a little while, and He who is coming will come and will not tarry. Now the just shall live by faith; but if anyone draws back, My soul has no pleasure in him." But we are not of those who draw back to perdition, but of those who believe to the saving of the soul (Hebrews 10:35-39).

The life of faith and obedience to Christ will bring us arrows of pain as well as arrows of victory. Such is the life of a true soldier in Jesus, but the rewards in this life and in the life to come are beyond measure. Press into Him and ask for grace sufficient for today. You and I are not alone in the walk of faith. There are those who have gone before us, and their lives shine as glorious examples of God's faithfulness and power in all things.

ENDNOTES

1. Lawrence K. Altman, "Parts of Africa Showing H.I.V. in 1 in 4 Adults," *New York Times On the Web*, June 24, 1998; quoting statistics of the latest country-by-country analysis led by Dr. Bernhard Schwartlander, U.N. epidemiologist. The results of the study were announced by Dr. Peter Piot, director of the U.N. AIDS Program on June 23, 1998, just prior to the 12th International AIDS Conference.

2. Anne Penketh, "AIDS and a lost generation: Children raising children." *The Independent Online Edition*, July, 14, 2006.

3. See Revelation 19:11-16; Hebrews 13:8.

4. See 2 Corinthians 3:18.

5. See 1 Peter 5:8.

6. Paraphrased from Ladislas Farago, *Patton: Ordeal and Triumph* (London: Barker, 1966).

EIGHT

Prayer Pioneers and the Facts of Fasting

To the irritation of some and the delight of others, the godly disciplines of prayer and fasting show up in every nook and cranny of God's Word and in the history of the Church. And everywhere you find prayer and fasting, you find victory in the midst of difficulty, the miraculous invading the impossible, and supernatural intervention permanently diverting natural intentions. In other words, God tends to show up in His glory and power whenever and wherever His people set themselves to pray and fast before Him.

Esther, the Jewish virgin who was chosen to replace Vashti as the queen of Persia and the wife of King Artaxerxes, called for all the Jews under Persian rule to join her in a solemn fast. She abstained from all food and drink for three days because the very life of her people was hanging in the balance (see Esther 4:16).

Faithful Anna, a widow of about 84 years who literally lived in the temple, devoted her life to prayer and fasting before God.

Even in those dark days, she was recognized and honored as a prophetess. As is so common with people whose lives are permeated by the disciplines of prayer and fasting, Anna walked up just as ancient Simeon had finished his prophecy over the infant Jesus.

Both Anna and Simeon lived in the timing and direction of God; their steps were literally established by the Lord. For Anna, the more than 80 long years of walking with God culminated in the moment she looked into the face of God incarnate and immediately began to proclaim the truth about God's chosen Son. How could such a woman walk up to total strangers and suddenly know that she was looking at God the Son? She never left God's house, but constantly *served God* with *fasting and prayer* night and day (see Luke 2:37). Most of us, on the other hand, get so busy with the affairs of life that the reality of Jesus grows dim. *We need to see Jesus afresh.* Anna clearly saw Jesus because she fasted and prayed. These things will also help us see Jesus more clearly.

Cornelius was a Roman centurion who commanded an elite band of Roman soldiers called "the Italian band," and he was a devout worshiper of God as well. Although he wasn't Jewish, he prayed constantly to the Lord, and his compassionate and extensive giving to the poor had won him a good reputation among the Jews in his area. He had an angelic visitation and was told to contact Peter the apostle. When Peter met Cornelius, the Gentile officer told him:

> *So Cornelius said, "Four days ago I was fasting until this hour; and at the ninth hour I prayed in my house, and*

behold, a man stood before me in bright clothing, and said, 'Cornelius, your prayer has been heard, and your alms are remembered in the sight of God'" (Acts 10:30-31).

Perhaps it was no accident that Cornelius, the first Gentile convert to Christ, was a Roman. God quickly demonstrated that His saving grace extended even to the two principal races involved in the crucifixion of His Son, and therefore to all races, tribes, and tongues. It is significant that Cornelius was constantly praying to God, and it was no accident that he received a supernatural visitation when he was *fasting and praying* before the Lord.

It was to this man who practiced the disciplines of prayer and fasting in his search for more of God that the mystery of the Gospel that *saves all humankind* regardless of race, color, culture, or sex was first preached. It was because Cornelius was praying and fasting *for more* that God chose him and his household to be the first ones in the Gentile kingdom to receive the baptism in the Holy Spirit with the evidence of speaking in tongues. The moral of this story is simple: If you want the anointing, pray and fast.

The *apostle Paul* and all the 276 Gentile passengers aboard the Alexandrian (Egyptian) ship headed toward Rome observed a full 14-day fast according to Acts chapter 27. When Julius, the Roman centurion in charge of Paul, was persuaded to sail against the advice of the apostle, the ship was nearly destroyed by a storm at sea. Only their obedience to Paul's Spirit-directed counsel saved their lives. It is clear from the context of the Bible record that it was Paul's prayer and fasting before God that saved all those lives and persuaded the Roman centurion to defy standard

Roman military procedure by ordering his soldiers to spare Paul's life instead of killing him during the crisis at sea.

Daniel's solitary fast and protracted prayer before God literally saved his nation and prevented demonic principalities from hindering God's purposes for Israel.

Ezra the prophet fasted before God when faced with an impossible task and an impossible situation.

Jesus, of course, fasted for 40 days and overcame the enemy's temptation before going forth *in the power of the Spirit* to launch His ministry and lay down His life for all people.

David fasted many times in his life as God transformed and transported him from the obscurity of a shepherd's life in his father's fields to the throne of Israel and Judah as God's greatest king outside of Jesus Christ, the King of kings.

Fasting is found throughout the Bible. It always seems to show up when ordinary people need extraordinary power, provision, and perseverance to overcome impossible odds, enemies, or obstructions.

Historically, revival breaks out when people seek God through prayer and fasting. The first worldwide missionary movement began in the first century in Acts 13. What was the context for this explosion of the Kingdom? As the Church *prayed and fasted*, God sent them out.

You will also find that *Polycarp*, in A.D.110, urged the believers to fast so that they could overcome temptations. *Tertulian* also defended fasting in A.D.210 as a great aid to religion. *Martin Luther* the reformer fasted as well. When he labored over the ancient manuscripts to translate the Scriptures into the German language, he combined his work with prayer and much fasting. I'm not surprised that Luther's German translation is one of the most accurate and inspiring Bible versions we have received. When I went to Germany, I had some people read it to me and translate it into English word-by-word, and there was something very special about it. *John Calvin* also fasted regularly, as did *John Knox.*

Virtually all the great evangelists fasted and prayed. *Charles Finney* wrote in his biography that he had frequent days of private fasting. He said that whenever he found the battery charge of the Spirit going down, when he felt the anointing of the Spirit weakening, he would go immediately into a three-day fast, and that he would always end those fasts feeling recharged.

Let me describe the results of that "battery charge." When Charles Finney would enter a city and start his meetings, people who entered the borders or boundaries of that city would start crying because a spirit of repentance would fall on them. When Finney would enter a warehouse, people throughout that factory would be slain in the Spirit wherever they were, whether they were saints or sinners. These events are recorded in the newspapers and journals of the day. The presence of God went with Finney in such power that people would come and get saved.

When *Jonathan Edwards* preached his famous sermon, "Sinners in the Hands of an Angry God," people in the audience said that they felt the ground open up and reveal the depths of hell, causing them to cry out to God for mercy and forgiveness. Edwards had combined his preparations and prayers with fasting.

John Wesley staunchly believed in fasting, and he personally fasted every Wednesday and Friday. He was so convinced that fasting should be a mandatory part of a minister's lifestyle that he told all his ministerial candidates that they would have to commit themselves to pray and fast every Wednesday and Friday if they wanted to minister with him, evangelize, or pastor a church founded through that movement. He became so powerful in his preaching that he became the primary voice in the Great Awakening and revival in England and the United States. Some historians say that the bloodshed and widespread suffering of the French Revolution that spread so quickly to the rest of Europe could easily have spread to England as well—except for Wesley's preaching. And Wesley gave much credit for the power and fruit of his ministry to the discipline of fasting before the Lord.

That great preacher and teacher, *Charles Haddon Spurgeon*, vigorously encouraged fasting, as did the American missionary to the Indians, *David Brainard. Rees Howells*, a great intercessor, regularly combined fasting with prayer.

Sadhu Sundar Singh was a Sikh and a devout Hindu "Sadhu" or holy man who was converted after receiving an open vision of Christ. He devoted his life to spreading the Gospel and became known as the "St. Paul of India and Tibet." He tried to observe a 40-day fast because Jesus had done it in the wilderness. Although he was unable to complete the full length of the fast, he said that the experience strengthened his spirit, allowing him to overcome all doubts, anger, and impatience. It was shortly after this fast that he first ventured into the Buddhist stronghold of Nepal to preach the Gospel.

So fasting has been common among great leaders through-out Church history, and it is required and expected of us by Jesus Christ. We don't fast to earn something; we fast to make a connection with our supernatural God. We are cleaning out the "pipe" that connects us to the anointing of God. It becomes corroded through the normal course of living in a fallen world, and the best way to cleanse our spiritual systems from the corrosion of sin and the world is through prayer and fasting. When doctors need to control an especially dangerous bacterial infection in their patients, they often employ a "one-two" punch of two complementary but different antibiotics at once to completely overwhelm the bacteria. God's dual-antibacterial treatment for the germs that assault our bodies is prayer combined with fasting.

Let me give you yet another brief list of the *benefits of fasting* before we go into the practical side of the fast.

When you fast:

1. *You are humbling yourself.*

2. *You will see life's priorities more clearly.* The Kingdom of God will become first in your life and you will get clarity concerning your values in life. (Like Mary, you will be able to choose "the good part" and set aside the bad—see Luke 10:42.)

3. *You will see balance return to areas of your life where there is imbalance.*

4. *Your selfish ambition and pride will begin to be washed away.* You'll start valuing and really appreciating the things that God has given you. You'll say, "Oh, this air is

so wonderful! It's so good to be alive!" Instead of complaining, "I will be happy only if I have a Mercedes Benz," you will notice a stronger appreciation for your family and for the simple basics like food, shelter, and good health. One thing is for sure: After your fast, the next time you eat a baked potato you'll say, "Thank You, Jesus."

5. *You will be more sensitive to God's Spirit, and the nine gifts of the Holy Spirit will work more effectively in your life.* Things will become very clear to you.

6. *Your hidden areas of weakness or susceptibility will rise to the surface so that God can deal with them.* I remember the time I was in the fifteenth day of a series of fasts, and was driving in Ft. Lauderdale, Florida, during what the locals called "the Yankee season." The term was coined to describe the flood of tourists who descended on that area from the northern states and particularly the Eastern seaboard. They tended to drive like they were still in a big, crowded city, complete with rude driving methods and profane gestures (the gestures bore no resemblance to the "One Way with Jesus" sign).

So I was on a fast when a driver who thought I wasn't moving fast enough rudely gave me "the signal." Something rose up in me and I started saying things that I *never* say! I was so ashamed that I said, "God! Lord, I thought I was a man of God. I repent, I didn't mean to say those things." And the Lord just seemed to chuckle as He let me know, "I'm cleansing you." When you fast, you will discover that hidden pockets of anger and bitterness, or other junk from which God wants to cleanse you, will come to the surface. Don't blame it on fasting and say, "When I fast I always get angry." God is cleansing you. It's an opportunity for physical and soulish poisons to come out of your system. Just give them to the Lord.

7. *God will make you more unselfish.* One of the things we need more of is self-control. Fasting will help you have self-control.

GOD'S WORD ABOUT FASTING

Legalism and a certain ignorance of the Scriptures have cloaked the biblical discipline of fasting in obscurity for most Christians. God wants to strip away the mystery and shed His light on this wonderful and simple tool for triumph. Most of the problems people have with fasting have to do with legalistic and rigid ideas of what a fast is and what it isn't. Many people think that if they don't fast 40 days like Jesus, then they just "aren't spiritual." If that is the case, then there have been very few so-called "spiritual" people in the Kingdom since the days that Jesus walked the earth. Most people will never be asked by God to observe a 40-day fast, and no one should feel guilty over such a thing.

Other people only think of a "total fast" when you mention fasting. In their minds, the only way to fast is to abstain from any liquids or food. In reality, this kind of fast is the rarest of all fasts, even in the Bible! In the area of fasting as much as in any other, this Bible promise is true: *"And you shall know the truth, and the truth shall make you free"* (John 8:32).

Following are some of the most commonly asked questions I receive about fasting and prayer:

How Long Is Long Enough?

I encourage you to fast one day a week if you can. Try to make it a water-only fast if possible, unless you have some physical problem. If that proves too difficult (for instance, you may work in an office or work environment where it is difficult to maintain your workflow on a water-only fast), then drink diluted (alkaline) fruit and vegetable juices. Begin after dinner in the evening and fast until dinner the next day. Or, if you have the grace, fast all the day through and break it after a full day at breakfast the next day. Make fasting a regular part of your life, and let the Lord deal with the areas of your soul that are hindering you from fulfilling your destiny in Him.

Why Do I Feel So Bad When Fasting Is So Good?

Nearly everyone experiences certain unpleasant side effects when beginning a fast. You may get a headache or feel slightly nauseated at first. This is because there are accumulated poisons stored in your body that are purged when you finally rest your intestines and stomach (this is a scientific fact). Even secular health authorities say that a one-day fast each week is very healthy for the human body—but it is also uncomfortable at times.

Will Fasting Cure Anything?

Fasting is not a cure-all. It *will* bring you into victory in the Spirit realm, but it does not mean you can fast and *still go on sinning*!

If someone who is committing adultery fasts and cries out to God, "Oh, Lord, give me deliverance!" but still commits adultery, that person will *not* be living in victory. You have to repent of your sins before you can be released from them. Fasting is not a cure-all from God; it is a weapon.

Never Fast to Impress Others

As I mentioned earlier, the Lord led me through 30 separate 40-day fasts over a period of almost 18 years. Throughout most of that time, *the Lord would not allow me to teach* on this subject or talk about my personal lifestyle. The only people who knew about the fasts were my wife and those who were in a "need-to-know" association with me. In the eighteenth year, the Lord said, "Now you can share about these fasts and impart this to others." Even then, I was only to share these things to help raise up an end-time army of people who will *fast and pray* so they can *do the works of Jesus* and *win victory* in the earth. But never was I authorized by the Lord to use my fasting experiences as a badge of honor to say, "Look, am I not spiritual? Look, I did this and I accomplished that!" If you want to obey God and begin to incorporate regular fasting in your life, then do it secretly as much as possible.

What If I Break My Fast in a Moment of Weakness?

Weakness is a natural part of the fasting discipline. In fact, that is the exact place we want our body and flesh to be. However, it can make things difficult on the job and at home sometimes. The first 19 times that I did 40-day fasts, I consumed nothing but water. Since I was carrying a full pastoral load at the time, sometimes I would get weak during the day. On the sixth or seventh day, I would drink a glass of fresh carrot juice. Six or seven days later, I would again drink another glass of carrot juice just to raise my strength levels for a time. (A 40-day fast is an extremely rigorous fast that should only be attempted by the direction and through the grace of God.)

When I observed my first 40-day fast in 1974 at the direction of the Lord, I was still a bachelor living in an apartment in Levelland, Texas, and was serving as the senior pastor of a church in that area. Now I love potato chips, even though they are not good for me. I made the mistake of buying a huge bag of my favorite kind of potato chips just before I started the fast. Every morning after I began the fast, I would get up and walk through the kitchen just sensing those potato chips calling out to me, "Hello, Mahesh. How are you? We are here. We are waiting for you. Mahesh, we are lonely—and we taste so good."

I just gritted my teeth and stayed on the fast. The problem was that with every new day, the appeals from the lonely potato chip bag grew more desperate. "Here we are. Crunchy. Salty." I rebuked them, I took authority over them, and I bound them; *but I did not cast them away.* On the eighteenth day of the fast, I broke! I ran into my kitchen, took a hold of that giant bag of potato chips, and ripped it open. I devoured every single potato chip right there in the kitchen. Then I turned to the Lord and said, "Lord, I am a wicked man. Forgive me, Lord." Then I went and continued with the fast and finished the 40 days.

A lady asked me one time after I shared this story, "Did you begin all over again?" I said, "Are you kidding!" I'm sharing this because I want you to remember that God has a sense of humor. If you set your sights on a three-day fast, but you only make it to the one and a half day point because you "followed" the McDonald's or Burger King sign you "saw in a vision," don't kick yourself too hard. You still accomplished much and God is pleased with your heart's desire for more of Him.

DIFFERENT TYPES OF FASTS

Most people are amazed to learn how many different kinds of fasts there are in the Bible and how many unique variations God has given Christian people in the modern era to accomplish the same thing! This knowledge can remove much of the mystery and frustration so many feel about the topic and discipline of fasting.

1. *The complete fast* refers to a total fast in which you eat nothing and drink nothing. The maximum time for this kind of fast is three days and nights. If you go any longer than three days without water (except in the literal presence of God), you face very serious health risks, including permanent damage to your key internal organs, and the cells in your body will begin to break down at a rapid pace. The *complete fast* is found in Ezra 8:21; 10:6 (called and observed by the prophet-priest Ezra) and in Esther 4:16 (called and observed by Queen Esther and the Jews in Sushan).[1] The complete fast is a fast of desperation, a fast of all-out hunger and urgency for the presence of God to come on the scene. It was this fast that Esther used to bring salvation to her nation and herself.

2. *The normal fast*, which Jesus observed in the wilderness, involves total abstention from food, but regular intake of water.

(If I am going to go on a fast, I also want to use that time to clean out my system; so I will drink distilled water. That is one of the best ways to flush all the poisons out of your system. You may want to squeeze some fresh lemon juice into the distilled water to increase the cleansing effect. If you are fasting for more than three days and you would like a slight pick-up, put a little honey in your water. You may prefer to drink herbal tea, but I would recommend that you avoid drinking heavily caffeinated beverages such as tea or coffee.

3. *The Daniel fast* or *partial fast* is what I recommend if you have never fasted before. Among the most well-known "fasters" in the Old Testament is Daniel. He describes one of his fasts in Daniel 10:2-3: "*In those days I, Daniel, was mourning three full weeks. I ate no pleasant food, no meat or wine came into my mouth, nor did I anoint myself at all, till three whole weeks were fulfilled.*" Daniel pleased and honored the Lord when he observed this fast. He ate "no pleasant meat" but instead ate vegetables and drank water. In First Kings 17, you will find that Elijah went on a partial fast of cakes made of meal and oil. John the Baptist was especially creative in his partial fast. He ate only locusts and honey, according to Matthew 3:4. God will honor a partial fast just as much as He will honor a total fast or complete fast. This fast is ideal for individuals with certain types of physical conditions such as diabetes, hypoglycemia, and anemia. It is also very practical for people who must work in physically or mentally demanding jobs while they are observing a fast.

4. *The group fast* or *corporate fast* is the kind of fast that turned God's wrath away from the wicked city of Nineveh in Jonah's day. Thousands of years later, the impact of this fast is still evident in modern-day Nineveh. It is the kind of fast Ezra called,

as well as Queen Esther. King Jehoshaphat called Judah to a fast (see 2 Chron. 20), and the prophet Joel called all the people of Israel to fast as well. A corporate fast is like a spiritual nuclear bomb, highly effective in breaking down the enemy's strongholds.

THINGS TO AVOID WHEN FASTING

When you are drinking fruit juices, avoid the acidic juices like orange juice or grapefruit juice because they can overwhelm your system. If you're drinking orange juice, I would dilute it to a ratio of about one-to-five. Make one-fifth of the drink juice and fill the glass with distilled water to keep it mild. Apple juice is good, but be careful not to overload your system with sugar—even the natural kind in fruit. In my experience, it can sap your strength and keep you feeling hungry. That is why you should dilute them. If you're on a real fast, believe me, your body will appreciate even that little bit of nourishment. Right now you may say, "Yuck, why dilute it?" But in the middle of a long fast, put four tablespoons of apple juice into a glass of water, and your body will get refreshment out of it.

Eliminate meats and desserts, and there will be times when you'll only want to eat fruits and nuts and vegetables. There are times when you go on a fast that, as a husband and wife, you may agree to abstain from sexual relationships. It is also very healthy for us to stop watching television as well as eating food during a fast. Spend that time in the Word and prayer. It's very practical.

CAN YOU FAST FOR MORE THAN ONE THING?

If you have many needs in your family or church, it may be necessary to fast and pray for them all at once. Write down the list of concerns or needs and offer them to the Lord in prayer.

Another question I hear often is, "How do you spend your time during the fast?" There is a place where you're not only fasting, but you *become* the fast. You almost become one with the fast. If you can pray, then pray. But if you aren't able to pray, then you become the fast before the Lord because you are living in that truth. And whenever it is time to pray, then pray.

At other times the Lord will give His own theme for the fast. The Lord will give pastors a theme for church-wide fasts. One time it might be repentance, and another time it might be evangelism where the entire church fasts and prays for souls. I will never forget the time the Lord gave me a very special theme for an individual fast. My father died when I was only five years old, and that left a void deep in my heart. The Lord told me, "I want to reveal to you My fatherhood, and I will become a father to you." The whole theme of that particular 40-day fast was the fatherhood of God, and it brought great peace, comfort, and fulfillment to me in a very important area.

RESPECT YOUR BODY IN THE FAST

There are times and seasons when you will feel weak during a fast, and it is very important that you respect your body during the fast. Don't abuse your body; respect it. My body has taken the Gospel into the remote regions of Africa and has brought hundreds of thousands to Jesus because it is healthy. If I had abused my body during those years of fasting, I wouldn't have been able to go into these places. When it is done with wisdom and care, fasting is actually a blessing for your body because it allows your digestive system to rest and purge residual poisons and toxins from your body.

How do you respect your body during a fast? If you feel physically weak after several days of fasting, sit down and rest a little. If you were running several miles a day before you began your fast, God *may* give you grace to do it when you fast. However, if you feel too weak to continue the running due to the fasting, then respect your body and wait until your fast is over to resume your running schedule.

One of the most important things we do during the fast is to tell our body "who is boss." When your body screams, "*I'm hungry,*" it's your job to say firmly, "Shut up." But don't be cruel to your body. Respect it, and once tamed, it will serve you and the Lord's purposes well.

THE TRUTH THAT MAKES A DIFFERENCE

I want to mention something that is very important when you enter a fast or pray to see a specific event or miracle come to pass. During a big conference in Nigeria for 4,000 pastors, I said, "I'm going to give you a truth that's going to release you. It's going to make a total difference in your ministry." They were wondering what it could possibly be, and I said, "I'm going to tell you this: '*You are not God.*'" I know it sounds simple and obvious, but if you are careful to remember this, then it will help you by reminding you *not to take on the responsibilities of God.* There are certain things I don't understand. For instance, I don't know why everyone does not get healed when we pray the prayer of faith in Jesus' name, but I have found peace in the truth revealed in Deuteronomy 29:29: "*The secret things belong to the Lord our God, but those things which are revealed belong to us and to our children forever....*"

START SMALL—MOVE TOWARD LONGER FASTS SLOWLY

Derek Prince was one of my primary teachers, and he taught me a great deal during our travels and ministry together. He shared with me that the longest fast he had observed at that time was a continuous fast of 14 days. Should I compare that with the 40-day fasts I've completed? No. Derek Prince was one of the most anointed ministers in the world, and had a disciplined life of fasting. He and his wife fasted every Wednesday of the year, and by the end of the year they had completed a 52-day fast. I'm sharing this to show you that the discipline of fasting is a very flexible discipline that is focused on intimacy with God, not some shallow performance-driven version of "putting in your time" with God.

God will give you the discipline to answer His call to the fast, but *start in moderation.* Don't begin immediately with a 21-day fast or a 40-day fast. It is just as scriptural for you to go on a 1-day fast. On Yom Kippur, the Jewish Day of Atonement, the children of Israel observed a 1-day fast. We've already looked at the 3-day fasts observed by Queen Esther and Ezra. Daniel also observed 3-day fasts as well as his more well-known 21-day partial fast (see Dan. 10:2-3). The longer 40-day fast was observed by Jesus, Elijah, and Moses.

If you plan to go on a fast and you have a medical problem like diabetes, are taking prescription medication, are pregnant, or are nursing, I encourage you to consult your physician before doing so. In general, however, everyone can go one day without food while drinking water or fruit and vegetable juices. Perhaps you can commit to limiting your food intake to one salad on the day you fast, or to eating only lentils or vegetables. There is great value in each of these kinds of fasts because you are putting the Lord and the things of His Kingdom first, and your body's appetites second.

What To Expect

I've already discussed the early symptoms most people experience during the first three days of a fast—headaches, nausea, and sometimes dizziness and a stiff neck. The good news is that once you press through the three-day barrier, you will begin to feel very good! By the time you reach the fourth or fifth day, you come into a realm of rest. You will find that you don't want to go back to eating, but once the fast is over you will feel hungry again. Then you will need to learn how to properly end the fast in a safe manner.

I encourage you to give some disciplined time to Bible reading and prayer during the fast, because you will also find that the devil will try to attack you in that time. He hates it when Christians fast and pray, and the spiritual battle can sometimes get intense, but there's victory ahead for your situation. Satan usually attacks us in the mental realm with a form of depression during a fast that manifests itself in a sense of heaviness. Just pray through to victory. Don't say, "Oh my, what's happening to me? Here I'm seeking the Lord and I'm depressed." Just take authority over the evil spirit that is attacking you. Expect spiritual attacks because you are committing an act of aggression against the devil's kingdom when you fast. He will try to hit back, but simply bind those things that he sends your way. Do warfare against them.

CHILDREN AND FASTING

It has been our experience that children can participate in modified fasting as they learn and grow in their faith. Our local body fasts corporately on a regular basis. This has offered an excellent opportunity to disciple our children in this grace. In a culture where fasting is a regular part of spiritual life, children are eager to be able to participate in the community. While nutrition and diet are important for growing children, there are numerous ways that they can find to walk in this discipline of humility, obedience and self-sacrifice. They may decide to fast from television, movies or video games. Others may give up desserts and junk food. I was touched to hear of one 8-year-old boy who asked if he could save his cookies, served as a snack during children's church, because he was fasting desserts as part of our corporate fast that was ending on the following day! He was not bound by religion or legalism, but was excited about and took seriously his part on the wall of prayer and fasting in our church. He understood that he was an integral part of our church body.

We have found that many families have testified to the power and unity they have experienced when they have participated in our corporate fasts as a family. Others have a regular fasting routine which their children all participate in as a matter of fact, just like brushing their teeth and reading the Bible. One family in our church will set aside one night per week to fast as a family during longer corporate fasts. Instead of dinner, they will spend that time worshiping and praying together. They each have a prayer focus, and at the end, they take communion together. During one corporate fast, their 6-year-old son asked,

"Is tonight the night that we have communion for dinner?" The kids love it, as the Lord always meets them in a special way.

As children get older, they have a greater concept of what fasting means and can begin to choose how and when they might want to fast. When one of our families needed a specific breakthrough in their business, they casually mentioned to their children to be praying about it. Later, their 11-year-old daughter came up and asked her mother, "Does Daddy still need new employees?" Then she asked, "What's a Daniel fast again?" Her mother told her it was fasting from meat and dessert. Her daughter said, "Well, I don't really like meat, but I love cheese. I should probably fast cheese too. I am going to go on a 3-day Daniel fast for Daddy to get the employees he needs." Immediately after the fast, her father got the exact number of employees he needed! It was unmistakably the result of his daughter's fast.

Including children in fasting is not just a ritual, but an opportunity to teach them the exponential power of fasting with the purpose of handing off this truth to the next generation. Our children are receiving an impartation of grace and seeing the testimony of the power that comes as we humble ourselves before the Lord in obedience to His Word.

BREAKING THE FAST WITH WISDOM

Exercise wisdom when you break your fast. This is especially important if you are breaking a fast that has gone on for seven or more days. Again, I urge you to treat your body kindly and with respect. I often hear people talking during corporate fasts who say, "I want the biggest steak in the world, and I also want the biggest baked potato in the world when I break this fast." If you do that, you will hurt your body. When you break a long fast, do so gradually. The real art to fasting with wisdom is to know how to *come into* the fast and how to *break* a fast. I recommend that you limit your first foods to small helpings of fresh fruit, some salad, vegetable broth, or some yogurt. You will learn after a while which is the best substance for you as you are breaking the fast.

Now we must move on to examine the incredible power of the corporate fast, and its role in the Lord's great end-time revival.

ENDNOTE

1. There is a biblical precedent for a supernatural 40-day fast without food *or water*. However, this fast was conducted in the *literal presence* of the glory of the Lord by Moses. Such a fast could be fatal under any other circumstances.

NINE

Corporate Prayer and End-Time Revival

The severe weather patterns we have seen wreaking havoc across the globe over the last decade or so have also given us prophetic insight into the changes taking place in the heavenly realm. Major storm patterns in the natural may signal an increase of activity in the spirit realm as well. Perhaps they are also a part of the earth's "labor pains" as it prepares for the appearing of Christ.[1]

The Lord wants to commend all those who have been strong and continued to exercise faith in the midst of storms. When Pearl Harbor was bombed by the Japanese air force in a surprise air attack, the American fleet in the harbor was left in shambles! America's response to this attack was to send forces to quell the enemy *at its root.*

In past years, intercessors who have obeyed the call to prayer have determined not to back off from the fight. This band of prayer warriors is pressing through much opposition and is taking back our divine inheritance from the enemy. Like so many recruits in the armed forces of our nation who thought they were joining the army to "see the world," perhaps many of us just joined up with Jesus to get a ticket out of hell. But we had unknowingly signed on the dotted line as an enlistee in a *holy army*!

The Body of Christ reminds me of an American movie released some years ago entitled, *Private Benjamin*. The central character in the movie is a woman who thinks she is going on a "cruise," but actually ends up in *boot camp*! Unfortunately, this "cruise mentality" also describes much of the activity and thinking of the Charismatic movement during much of the 1980s and '90s. The season has changed.

Revival is in the land, and a new hunger is beginning to sweep across the nations of the world. The Lord is speaking a new prophetic word about an old prophetic word. The old word is "Pray!" The new word is, "*Pray corporately!*"

The Lord is opening our eyes to the simple truth that prayer is where everything begins and ends in the realm of the Spirit. It is here that everything is accomplished. Prayer is the true genetic code of the Church. We have received other mutant genes that have caused us to evolve away from God's true design for His Body. *Nothing that God is going to do will happen without prayer.*

I've heard people say that they were called to preach, to lay hands on the sick, to evangelize, and so forth, but they would quickly add, "But I'm not called to intercession." The truth is that we should not be ministering to others if we have not spent time communing with and receiving from the One who ordains the anointing for all ministry.

Anna the prophetess, a widow from her young years, came continually to the temple to minister to the Lord in prayer and fasting. Her intercession played a key role in bringing forth the Messiah. *Anna knew Him.* Tragedy in her life caused her to become intimate with the Lord in prayer. Do you know Him? We can have the gifts of the Spirit, the power to impart them, do miracles, and cast out demons, and still hear Jesus say at the end of the age, *"Depart from Me, I never knew you!"* (see Matt. 7:23).

THE POWER OF HARMONIOUS PRAYER

Again I tell you, if two of you on earth agree (harmonize together, make a symphony together) about whatever [anything and everything] they may ask, it will come to pass and be done for them by My Father in heaven (Matthew 18:19 AMP).

Jesus said that if two of us will harmonize together as touching any thing, *it shall be done for us!* God is calling the Church today to corporate prayer and intimate communion with Him. He will know us because we have known Him in the place of prayer (see Matt. 25:23). God's altar of prayer is open to us at all times. The Lord has given us a powerful tool in the Spirit for the work of prayer: *prayer languages.* As we move ahead in corporate prayer, the Spirit will give us new and powerful tongues that will leave a tremendous spiritual deposit in our lives and change the destiny of nations. As a few good men stand in cooperation with the Holy Spirit, He will raise up a standard like a flood against the enemy.

"WATCHING"—PART OF EVERY GREAT REVIVAL

Since beginning The Watch of the Lord™ in Charlotte, North Carolina, in 1995, the Holy Spirit has moved on our prayers and changed every life that has been involved with The Watch.[2] The very biblical practice of "watching" is a historical part of every great ministry and every great revival. An excerpt from John Wesley's journal of 1739 reads:

"Mr. Hall, Kitchen, Ingram, Whitfield, Hutchins, and my brother Charles were present at our love feast at Fetter Lane with about 60 of our brethren. At about 3:00 in the morning as we were continuing instant in prayer, the power of God came mightily upon us so much that many cried out for exceeding joy and many fell to the ground. As soon as we recovered a little from the awe and amazement of His majesty, we broke out with one voice, 'We praise Thee, oh God! We acknowledge Thee to be the Lord!'"[3]

Joel and the people of Israel, Wesley, the Moravians, and other groups have pioneered in all-night prayer. They tilled the ground and planted the seeds of God's heart for corporate prayer. God is now watering the seeds of revival and raising up new watchmen to reap *a new harvest through prayer*. The Lord's breath is blowing, causing corporate prayer to spring forth across the earth.

The enemy hates prayer, particularly corporate prayer, because he knows that *when two or more will come in agreement with the Holy Spirit, the devil will lose every time* (see Matt. 18:19). Satan's main strategy is to *divide and conquer*. Jesus said, *"Every kingdom divided against itself is brought to desolation, and a house divided against a house falls*" (Luke 11:17b). The love of Jesus is always available to us to heal our hurts and minister to our needs, but there is more to the picture.

He has intended for us to be involved with a corporate community, harmonizing together in a lifestyle of corporate communion and prayer. This call involves sacrifice. I believe that those who don't respond to this call are going to miss something crucial in our generation. In Luke chapter 18, the persistent widow demonstrates the power of persistent, insistent, and focused prayer:

> *Then He spoke a parable to them, that **men always ought to pray and not lose heart**, saying: "There was in a certain city a judge who did not fear God nor regard man. Now there was a widow in that city; and she came to him, saying, '**Get justice for me from my adversary.**' And he would not for a while; but afterward he said within himself, 'Though I do not fear God nor regard man, yet **because this widow troubles me I will avenge her**, lest by her continual coming she weary me.' " Then the Lord said, "Hear what the unjust judge said. And **shall God not avenge His own elect who cry out day and night** to Him, though He bears long with them? I tell you that **He will avenge them speedily.** Nevertheless, when the Son of Man comes, will He really find faith on the earth?"* (Luke 18:1-8)

PERSISTENT PRAYER AND GOD'S FAVOR

The persistent widow in this parable came to the unrighteous judge, pleading with him day after day until he gave her what she wanted. The One we are coming to is the *righteous*

Judge. How much more will He give His favor to those who are persistent in prayer? His benevolent heart toward us is only lightly foreshadowed in the response of King Xerxes toward Esther. He is telling us to ask for the Kingdom. He is saying this about our generation: "You write the decree in prayer."

Jesus asked an amazing question related to persistence in prayer: "*When the Son of Man comes, will He **really find faith** on the earth?*" (Luke 18:8). In other words, Jesus is saying that your faith is expressed by your prayer life.

In Isaiah 59, we find the people of God spiritually destitute as the prophet writes:

> *Therefore justice is far from us, nor does righteousness overtake us; we look for light, but there is darkness! For brightness, but we walk in blackness! We grope for the wall like the blind, and we grope as if we had no eyes; we stumble at noonday as at twilight; we are as dead men in desolate places* (Isaiah 59:9-10).

The Lord was displeased that the people could find nothing but darkness. The prophet says in Isaiah 59:16, "He saw that there was no man, and wondered that there was no intercessor; therefore His own arm brought salvation for Him; and His own righteousness, it sustained Him." The Lord was amazed that no one was seeking Him and interceding for the people of God. Three verses later we read, "So shall they fear the name of the Lord from the west, and His glory from the rising of the sun; when the enemy comes in like a flood, the Spirit of the Lord will lift up a standard against him" (Isa. 59:19).

I believe the Lord has sovereignly seen the Church in the nations groping in the darkness, seeking the light. Now He has decided to move, to take things in His own mighty hands. The Spirit of the Lord is raising up a standard against the flood of evil from the mouth of the enemy. We see this pictured in the opposition against the end-time church in Revelation 12:15. The Lord reaches certain times where He says, "Enough! I'll have mercy!" That is when He pours out His Spirit. Just as He parted the Red Sea for the oppressed and enslaved people of God to bring them up from Egypt, He is parting our "Red Sea" today to deliver us from the pursuit of the enemy.

GOD IS SEARCHING FOR THE "GREAT WALL OF PRAYER"

The Lord is saying, "Forget about 'your' ministry and 'your' gifts. Forget about finances. Forget about wanting to get married. *It is time to seek Me!*" (see Matt. 6:33). Respond to the call of God and make room in your life for corporate prayer. Just as the only structure that can be seen on earth by standard weather satellites is the Great Wall of China, I believe that the work the Lord wants to see when He looks down on the earth is a great wall of prayer that stretches around the world. It is time for the watchers to take their place on that wall!

There isn't one historical revival that was not ushered in by intercessors gathering in prayer to tarry before the living God. These intercessors refused to let the standard fall to the ground—no matter how much they had to sacrifice, just like those few good men at the battle of Iwo Jima who sacrificed all to raise the United States flag on a strategic hill of advantage, signaling victory over the Japanese forces there.

The Word of the Lord to the New Testament believers was to *tarry in prayer until the power of the Holy Spirit came!*[4] Ezra the prophet records an historic prayer of Jews in exile who longed for revival and the opportunity to repair the wall and rebuild the ruins of their destiny:

> *And now for a little while grace has been shown from the Lord our God, to leave us a remnant to escape, and to give us a peg in His holy place, that our God may enlighten our eyes and give us a measure of revival in our bondage. For we were slaves. Yet our God did not forsake us in our bondage; but He extended mercy to us in the sight of the kings of Persia, to revive us, to repair the house of our God, to rebuild its ruins, and to give us a wall in Judah and Jerusalem* (Ezra 9:8-9).

TIME TO TAKE BACK THE WALL!

Amos the prophet asked the question, *"Can two walk together, unless they are agreed?"* (Amos 3:3). God is calling the Church to get into step with Him, to harmonize in prayer, and to come into total agreement with His purposes. The Church has inundated people with programs and teachings to promote unity, but these attempts have been futile. Why? Because people cannot be "taught" or "programmed" into unity. It is a supernatural act that can be done only by the Spirit as all hearts focus on Jesus Christ. As we noted earlier in this chapter, Jesus Himself gave us the key to answered prayer in the Gospel of Matthew:

> *Again I tell you, if two of you on earth agree (harmonize together, make a symphony together) about whatever [anything and everything] they may ask, it will come to pass*

and be done for them by My Father in heaven (Matthew 18:19 AMP).

The Lord's new word on corporate prayer *has nothing to do with following programs, agendas, or the thinking of people.* It has everything to do with being involved in Spirit-led submitted prayer. Our task is simply to come together and *harmonize* in prayer and worship in God's presence, offering ourselves to Him in love and adoration; while making ourselves available to stand in the gap for others, to obey His every instruction, and then to simply wait until He shows up.

Every prayer led by the Spirit will touch the heart of God. If God's Word is true, then the Holy Spirit really does make intercession for us when we don't know how to pray, according to Romans 8:26. God is opening this window for corporate prayer, and we must go through while it is open. If we do, revival will sweep across the earth as never before. If we don't, I believe it will leave a breach so wide that the enemy will rush through.

The Lord's house is the house of prayer. His "address" is prayer (see Matt. 21:13; Isa. 56:7). If you want to be with Him, then you must meet Him at His house, the house of prayer. Jesus walked into the corporate expression of religion in His day and saw that the people were doing everything *but praying.* They were buying, selling, and conversing, and had even made the temple an extension of the street or a shortcut for carrying their goods from one place to another! He took one look and said, "I don't live here. My house is called a house of prayer!" If we want to be where God is, then we must be in the place of corporate prayer.

Jesus was a *man of prayer* before everything else. Every response He made to the people around Him was solely at the direction He received from the Father in prayer! Jesus said, "Most assuredly, I say to you, the Son can do nothing of Himself, but what He sees the Father do; for whatever He does, the Son also does in like manner" (John 5:19). The victory Jesus Christ won at the Cross was first won in the place of fervent prayer in Gethsemane—while the disciples slept through it!

In the fall of 1994, the Holy Spirit birthed a "spiritual baby" in our local fellowship that is now loved by thousands of people in the Body of Christ around the world. This spiritual "baby" is corporate prayer and is called The Watch of the Lord. Its roots are ancient and holy, coming ultimately from the very heart of God, who said, "*For My house shall be called a house of prayer for all nations*" (Isa. 56:7b). Perhaps you have been in the same place as the woman in the Song of Solomon who said, "Well, God's not coming. I'm going to bed" (see Song of Sol. 5:2-4). Suddenly there is a knock on the door, and the Lord is waiting for you to open it. Fasting is the key to corporate prayer.

EXCHANGE INDEPENDENCE FOR INTERDEPENDENCE

The time has come for us to exchange our independence for *interdependence*. Independence tends to make people vulnerable to deception, particularly when they begin to move in supernatural revelation and gifts. It is of primary importance that our ministry flows out of the context of the family of God.

In Second Chronicles 20, King Jehoshaphat wasn't content to merely pray to God on his own. He knew the stakes were too high, the danger too great for solo prayer. He not only "set himself to seek the Lord" but also proclaimed a nationwide time of fasting and prayer. As a result of Judah's corporate obedience in prayer and fasting, God answered with supernatural deliverance.

If the nations are to be harvested and the high places of iniquity are to be pulled down, *it will be through corporate prayer*! If we are going to fulfill the destiny that the Lord has given us as churches and nations, *it will be through corporate prayer*.

In Solomon's day, it was corporate prayer that moved the hand of God against Israel's enemies. God's prescription for deliverance from the destitution in Joel's time was to bring the people, great and small, to seek the Lord in prayer through the night. According to the prophet, God said, "*Consecrate a fast, call a sacred assembly; gather the elders and all the inhabitants of the land into the house of the Lord your God, and cry out to the Lord*" (Joel 1:14). As the people of God humble themselves before Him in prayer, God says, "*...I will hear from heaven, and will forgive their sin and heal their land*" (2 Chron. 7:14).

HARMONIOUS CORPORATE PRAYER IS POWERFUL

When you come together with brothers and sisters to spend hours in consistent, concentrated, corporate harmony with the Holy Spirit, things will begin to change. He will change your perspective, your endurance levels, your patience, and many other areas as well. Corporate prayer is a very practical "discipling tool" in the life of the local Body of Christ. When Peter was released from prison by the angel, it was because the church at Jerusalem was conducting an all-night prayer meeting on his behalf! (See Acts 12:1-12.) It was after an extended period of harmonious corporate prayer that the Holy Spirit fell on those waiting in the upper room on the Day of Pentecost (see Acts 2:1-4).

Corporate prayer will mysteriously and supernaturally break down dividing walls in the Body of Christ, transcending denominational lines. As Christians, you and I need to be on the battlefield, presenting ourselves to God as a company of prayer warriors committed to pushing back the enemy and raising God's standard over our land! It is time for you to take your place on the wall of corporate prayer.

God releases an awesome authority to us when several people come together in His name to fast and pray. This authority contains the kind of power that can dislodge mountains! It is a weapon God has given us so we can break every satanic curse and stronghold over our lives, our families, our churches, our cities, and our nation! It happens when we *choose* to join our spiritual dynamic energies together as one "laser beam," if you will, of God-given power and concentrated heavenly light.

In late August 1995, two watchmen dreamed about Paris, France, during the same week. A third had a clear impression of children's school lunch boxes and desks. On Friday, September 1, 1995, as The Watch pursued these impressions in prayer, we believed there was a plot by Jihadist terrorists to bomb a Jewish school near Paris. We prayed the plot would be completely foiled. The following Friday, the Associated Press wire service reported an attack on a French elementary school on Thursday, September 7.[5]

The extremists had set a car bomb to explode outside a Jewish school in Villeurbane, France, at the moment the students left school in the afternoon. The Rabbi of the school reported that for the first time in the school's 70-year history the school clock stuck. Miraculously, the clock hands stopped just three minutes before the bell and prevented the children from exiting into the yard at the time the bomb was detonated. The bomb exploded without injury to the 700 children who were still inside. Consistent, committed, corporate fasting and prayer had trained these watchmen how to hear the Lord and to focus their prayers to destroy the works of the enemy.

Let me ask you a conceptual question to help you understand the power of corporate prayer and fasting. If one laser beam is powerful enough to cut through hardened steel at close to the speed of light, what could 21, 50, or 100 laser beams do if their power was gathered together into one concentrated beam of power? That is a good picture of *our power* in corporate fasting and prayer! God has literally given us the power and the commission to blow open strongholds, tear down kingdoms of darkness, and break every dark curse over our families in His mighty name!

RESHAPE HISTORY THROUGH CORPORATE FASTING AND PRAYER

Remember that Jesus is sending you and me into the world just as the Father sent Him—except that *He is sending us out together*. God birthed a miracle almost 2,000 years ago in the city of Jerusalem when He began to pour out His Spirit upon all flesh. In that moment, the Church was born; and an anointed army full of the Holy Ghost was unleashed upon the world and the kingdom of darkness. Now as never before, it is time for us to rise up in God's glory and descend upon city after city and nation after nation, taking the Gospel of peace into the kingdom of darkness. Only one thing can come from our obedience: We will literally change the destiny of humanity everywhere we go! I believe in the canon of revealed Scripture. I also believe that we have the opportunity by God's grace to write a second "book of the acts" of the apostles in our day as we go forth in power to do mighty exploits in Jesus' name!

God wants to impart His vision of worldwide harvest to us so that we will look beyond ourselves to the fields that are white for harvest. You and I received the good news of Jesus for more than our own salvation.

We have a responsibility in Christ to reshape history and transform the destiny of our churches, our cities, and the nations. This is the vision of Jesus and the commission of the Father.

The only way we can presume to reshape history is to pray and fast for God to reveal His glory to the nations. We need to allow the passion of God to possess our souls and direct our prayers in intercession. When Derek Prince and I went as an apostolic team to Pakistan some years ago, we literally saw God work many wonderful miracles.

On our way to a morning meeting, we passed by an elderly blind woman, her empty eye-sockets testifying to the fact that she had been born without eyes. She sat daily by the open sewer to beg beside the busy road. "Mahesh, take her picture," Brother Derek said. For us this poor woman represented countless souls around the world who sit in the darkness waiting for the light of Christ. Her picture was engraved on my heart. I silently prayed, "Holy Spirit, here we are in this dark country, which is among the poorest of the poor. Show them that Jesus is the Son of God and that He is King of kings."

That night during the service, the Holy Spirit led me to take authority over the powers of darkness surrounding that city. As I bound the spirit of antichrist, a demonic roar came from the sky. Suddenly a thunderclap of the victory of Jesus sounded. In a moment, a figure emerged from the middle of the crowd. It was the woman we had taken a picture of that morning! With a shining face and the bluest eyes you've ever seen in the place where there had been only eye sockets, she pointed at me and said, "As this man prayed I saw a flash of light. Now I can see!"

FIRST YOU MUST BIND THE STRONGMAN

I am sharing this story to show you the *major key for this success*—and it goes back to the time the Lord implanted the truth of prayer and fasting in my life. Before I ever went into nations such as Pakistan, Zambia, Zaire, and Haiti, I *fasted and prayed and did aggressive spiritual warfare.* Long before I ever stepped onto the soil of Pakistan, I did battle by the Spirit against the power of the antichrist. *Before* I ever entered the region of Central Africa to minister to the people of Zaire or Zambia, I did battle against the power of sorcery and witchcraft in those places. First you must bind the strongman; then you can loot his house! (See Luke 11:21-22.) The major "key to the city" and the "key to the nations" in my ministry and in yours in this end-time revival is fasting and prayer.

I submit to you that if your family, ministry, or church is confronting unseen obstacles; if unseen powers of darkness are resisting or tormenting your family or church; you can go beyond victory to triumph if you will only take up the special weapon that God has placed in your Holy Ghost arsenal. God wants you to go forth in a new and special anointing, but it will only come through prayer and fasting.

One of the things we are all commissioned to do is to pray that the Lord would give us souls, corporately and individually. We must ask the Lord of the harvest to impart to us the spirit of evangelism and to bring upon us unusual signs and wonders to confirm our faithful preaching of His Word. It is through prayer that souls are "birthed" into the Kingdom of God.

THE AMERICAN INDIAN VISION

During numerous 40-day fasts, there were seasons when a heavenly atmosphere would surround me and revelation would come that was quite supernatural.

In the last seven days of one of these 40-day fasts, I was feeling very weak. One day my work schedule was full and I was already tired, with an evening service still awaiting me that evening. I tried to rest before the meeting. I was neither asleep nor completely awake, but I literally saw an American Indian in the room. I could see him so clearly that I can still describe his long black hair in pigtails, his handsome face, his vest, and the beautiful Indian jewelry he wore. He asked me, "Where is the water? I am so thirsty."

Then I heard a voice other than my own tell him, "There is water *that way*." In that moment, he began to run and passed from my sight. When I saw him again, he was coming toward me, and he looked like he had traveled a long way through desert regions and had fought through cactus because his handsome face was torn by thorns. He still had not found any water, and he was dying of thirst. I heard the Lord say to me, "Give him water," and I knew that God wanted me to give this American Indian the water of life. I was amazed because the man and the events in the open vision were so real to me.

When I went to the evening meeting at the church, even during the time of worship, I still felt like I was in that vision. I told the people, "I had an open vision of the Lord in which I saw an American Indian man." Then I described the Indian in detail, mentioning his sleek black hair, the exact shape of his nose, his hand-tooled belt with the big jeweled buckle, the beautiful Indian jewelry he wore, and his overpowering thirst for water. When I finished describing what I saw, I said, "God wants us to give living waters to every tribe and people in the world."

Suddenly a holy hush descended in the congregation because in that instant a handsome American Indian walked into the room, wearing a vest and beautiful Indian jewelry! He was a total stranger, but he did not sit down as you would expect. He walked right down the center of the auditorium and all the way up to the altar and said, "I need Jesus." He gave his life to the Lord right there in front of the congregation only seconds after I'd described the vision I'd received from the Lord.

Afterward I learned the rest of this man's story. He was from an Indian tribe that was based primarily in Missouri. He made Indian jewelry and set up his business in malls and shopping centers around the country. He was separated from his wife, had been living in sin, and was crying out to the Lord for answers for his life. This man was driving through our state to set up his mobile jewelry shop in some shopping malls in the region when he passed by our building and saw a golden light shining around it. The building didn't have a steeple or a sign that indicated to him that it was a church, but he saw the golden glow so he turned in and parked his vehicle. When he heard us worshiping God, he realized it was a church and decided to come in. After he was saved, the man arranged to have his estranged wife come to him, and two days later I was privileged to baptize both of them in water. They were both baptized in the Holy Spirit, and God gloriously healed their marriage. This precious Native American truly received living water!

REVELATION TRUTH AT EVERY LEVEL

Revelation comes as we pray and fast, and when God speaks, His revelation is true *at every level*. It will be true in the natural, it will be true in the spiritual, it will be true in the realm of the soul, and it will be true historically. For instance, there are many prophetic words about Israel that are also true for the Church, or at the very least also provide blessings for God's spiritual Israel because the Lord's Word is *truth*. On every level in which you encounter His Word, the truth will be there.

God spoke to my heart through the miracle of the American Indian vision and said, "I want to pour out My Spirit; I want to give water to every thirsty soul. There are people who are thirsting for true life. Go out and win the lost tribes. Go to all the people, to every tribe and ethnic group. I want to pour out My living water for them. They are thirsty; they are dying. Give them the true living waters of the Holy Spirit. I am commissioning you.

The Church is to give the living waters to those who are dying of thirst."

That prophetic word was true on a global level, and it was also true at the individual level when I saw that one American Indian man who was thirsty for God's Spirit. The Lord made His prophetic word come to pass in one man's life that night in the church service, and His Word is true on a worldwide level too. As the Bible declares, "...*let God be true but every man a liar*" (Rom. 3:4a).

If you examine the Word of God, you will find that it is true at every level. His Word on healing can be applied the same way. He has promised us healing for our souls, bodies, marriages, churches, cities, and nations. *If we seek Him*, the healing Word will come and accomplish that for which it was sent.

The Lord has promised that when we cry out, fast, and pray for the rain of His blessing, He will answer. "Lord, we don't want our country to miss Your precious rain. We desperately need both the former and the latter rain." If we don't cry out for God's rain, then our nation will burn for other things—unholy and destructive things. Today our nation is burning with lust and unrighteousness, and the Lord wants to pour out His rain of righteousness, holiness, and glory. But if His people won't cry out, to whom will He turn?

[God] *saw that there was no man, and wondered that there was no intercessor...* (Isaiah 59:16).

I believe the Lord has prepared a worldwide outpouring of His Holy Spirit for His Church for these last days. It is God's supernatural answer to the desperate needs and end-time pressures that are upon us. Now it is our turn to seek Him, to cry out for Him, to pray and fast for His visitation of glory.

GLOBAL HARVEST REQUIRES GLOBAL MAGNITUDE PRAYER

Just as Jesus prays and intercedes for us day and night without ceasing, so should we intercede for the lost and for laborers for the harvest. This great harvest is global in magnitude. Therefore it requires corporate prayer on the same magnitude. When a wheat farmer wants to harvest half an acre of grain, he only needs to plan on bringing in a limited amount of machinery and just a few workers. However, when he wants to harvest 100,000 acres in a day, he has to plan to bring a large number of combines, many skilled operators, and an army of workers, or all is lost.

God is calling the Church worldwide to corporate prayer and fasting as never before, and it is because we face an imminent harvest of monumental, global proportions! It is time for us to answer God's call to prayer and fasting as one people, united around our one Savior, one faith, and one Lord.

ENDNOTES

1. See Romans 8:22-23.

2. The Watch of the Lord™ began in January 1995 when the Lord said to us, "Watch with Me." In response we invited about 20 people to spend from 10 P.M. Friday until 6 A.M. Saturday keeping the "night watch," which is going without sleep for spiritual reasons. We waited on God in worship and prayer, and shared in communion through Jesus' body and blood represented in the Lord's Supper. Every Friday since, for over a decade, we have done the same.

Now The Watch is a global movement of corporate prayer. Watch groups have sprung up throughout the United States and around the world. We are experiencing the power that is unleashed through the harmonizing of a body of believers in consistent prayer and fasting. We find ourselves in the midst of a renewed visitation that is manifesting the glory of the Lord with signs, wonders, and miracles! If you are interested in beginning a Watch of the Lord in your local fellowship, contact Mahesh Chavda Ministries, at P.O. Box 411008, Charlotte, NC, 28241, or call 704-543-7272. You may also contact us online at www.maheshchavda.com to find resources and helpful articles or to join our services by live webcast from our watch headquarters in Charlotte every Friday night.

3. John Wesley, *Journal II*, 1739.

4. See Luke 24:49.

5. Associated Press, "14 Hurt by Bomb at French School," Villeurbane, France, September 8, 1995.

Chapter Ten

How to Release the Apostolic Anointing

I love to read the Book of Acts because it is God's journal of the first time He poured out His wonderful Spirit upon all flesh and released apostolic ministry into the earth. The world still hasn't recovered from the *first time* God did it, and now He is about to do it *again* with a great flood of His glory and anointing. I believe you and I were born "for such a time as this."

We are on the edge of a history-making move of God among the nations of the earth. But we have to do something to prepare for it *before it comes*. God's glory in us is like precious gold or silver ore closely held by granite or other structures of stone. The stones must be broken up into tiny pieces and then subjected to the celestial fires of God so His precious elements may be released in purity and glory to dazzle the eyes of the world.

What could turn up the "heat" of God's presence in our lives to burn away the dross and leave only the purest of gold? What could break down the rocky places in our hearts so the "God in us" can flow effortlessly out of our lives to the poverty-stricken world around us? What is this "crucible of the anointing" that is able to transform piles of rocky gold ore into priceless golden ingots and treasures of apostolic passion and apostolic ministry? The New Testament pattern for the release of apostolic anointing and power is seen in the Book of Acts:

> *Now in the church that was at Antioch there were certain prophets and teachers: Barnabas, Simeon who was called Niger, Lucius of Cyrene, Manaen who had been brought up with Herod the tetrarch, and Saul. As they ministered to the Lord and fasted, the Holy Spirit said, "Now separate to Me Barnabas and Saul for the work to which I have called them." Then, having fasted and prayed, and laid hands on them, they sent them away. So, being sent out by the Holy Spirit, they went down to Seleucia, and from there they sailed to Cyprus (Acts 13:1-4).*

What is the "crucible" in which the apostolic ministry was released in the first century? It is clearly released in the context of the Church praying fervently and fasting corporately. It is in this atmosphere that the Holy Spirit clearly speaks with very specific and definite direction. It was in obedience to specific direction from the Holy Spirit that the church leaders at Antioch laid hands on Barnabas and Saul "having fasted and prayed." What does this mean for us today?

NEWSFLASH: GOD (AND HIS GIFTS) ARE SUPERNATURAL

For centuries, the Church has lumbered along at half speed on the ministry of only three of the five *doma* or equipping gifts

God originally intended for it to have. The ministry offices of the apostle and the prophet were generally rejected as having "passed away" with the death of the original apostles, while the offices of evangelist, pastor, and teacher somehow escaped the "grave" that claimed the first two. The results are as predictable as if someone decided your six-cylinder vehicle would run better if you unplugged two or three of your spark plugs as "unnecessary."

To make matters worse, nearly every one of the nine supernatural *charis* gifts listed by the apostle Paul in First Corinthians 12 were also dismissed as no longer "necessary," and were considered to have "passed away" with the apostles and prophets as well! Despite the immanent wisdom of man, God didn't make a mistake, and He said what He said in the Book of Ephesians, in First Corinthians 12, and in Romans 12 for a very specific reason. God Himself and revival are, by definition, *supernatural*. So no matter how uncomfortable men and women may be with the supernatural, God will forever remain just that—as will His gifts.

History documents that virtually every great revival and awakening in the world has been led by anointed leaders whose passionate ministries were accompanied by supernatural signs and wonders, as well as the full range of the charismatic gifts of the Spirit. The great revival we see rising up today is no exception. We urgently need apostolic power, authority, and leadership abilities during this great worldwide harvest.

For this reason, God is calling the end-time Church *into the fullness of the fivefold ministry*. We need to be running on "all cylinders" if God's glory is to truly cover the earth. We can no longer be content to limp along without the oversight of the apostolic office or the insight and vision of the prophetic office of the Church. We need every single charismatic gift God has for us to keep the Church strong, healthy, inspired, and holy. The only way this can happen is for the Church to turn up the fires of God through persistent corporate fasting and prayer! This will create an atmosphere or crucible of glory that will superheat and purify our lives and ultimately release the apostolic anointing into the Church and the world.

In this revival, signs and wonders will instantly destroy decades, and even centuries, of the enemy's evil works of bondage in one moment, releasing hundreds of thousands to receive Christ as Lord in one night! This can only happen through the *power of the Spirit*. We thank God the Father for the anointing, but He is calling us to go deeper into Him through fasting and prayer. Then He can entrust and empower us with the same *power* of the Spirit He gave His Son, Jesus Christ, after His 40 days of fasting in the wilderness.

God's Power and the Sorcerers' Tree

I remember the time I was conducting a mass evangelism campaign in the city of Kananga, Zaire, an area gripped by sorcery. This outreach conducted by our ministry was the first ever held in that area by those filled with the power of the Holy Spirit, and things were going well. This was despite the aggressive opposition of powerful witch doctors who had dominated that area for many years. Right from the start, they came to publicly pronounce curses on us. Most of the people feared these servants of satan. I was told by the people there, "These witch doctors have power to tell someone, 'You will die in seven days,' and the person will drop dead on the seventh day."

Our meetings made these witch doctors so angry that they called in every witch doctor in the whole region for a meeting to figure out how to stop us from proclaiming Christ. They gathered together beneath the branches of a towering tree used by sorcerers for many generations. They believed that spiritual power for evil emanated from this "sorcerers' tree;" and it was here that the witch doctors conducted evil ceremonies and ate human flesh as they cast evil spells on our evangelistic meetings being held some miles away.

On the final night of the outreach, the sorcerers again gathered beneath the "magic" sorcerers' tree to conduct demonic worship and rituals. These men and women were completely given over to the darkness of satan, and they angrily cursed the Christians, ate human flesh, and discussed plans on how to stop the meetings (since nothing they had already tried was working).

At the end of my message that evening, the Lord told me to break the yoke of witchcraft over that region and loose the people from its power. While the sorcerers raged beneath their "incantation" tree, I declared before the thousands of people gathered there, "Satan, I bind you. I take authority over the spirit of witchcraft, and I break the curse of sorcery over this area!"

In that moment, according to the reports of several eyewitnesses from the area where the witch doctors were gathered, flames of fire streaked across the sky, spanning the approximately seven-to-eight-mile distance from the site of our meeting to fall upon the sorcerers' tree. The fire instantly set the tree ablaze. The branches, which were spread 34 feet across, were *consumed from the top down*! It did not split the trunk or branches as would normally happen to a tree struck by lightning. This tree trunk burned for *three days* until it was consumed down to the height of a man's head. It still stands today like a burnt match stick, a mute reminder of the power of the name of Jesus!

We learned about the details of this miracle from some of the sorcerers themselves! They said that when the fire came down and ignited the sorcerers' tree, some of the witch doctors were blinded, some were burned, and some of them repented when they saw the overwhelming power of God. They came to us with the story and asked us how to be saved![1]

When I visited the site of the sorcerer's tree and stood before the charred trunk marking all that remained of satan's evil grip on that area, I was reminded of Elijah's confrontation with the prophets of Baal in First Kings 18. My spirit leapt within me, and I cried out as did Elisha of old when the mantle of anointing fell on him, "…*Where is the Lord God of Elijah?*" (2 Kings 2:14).

Elisha was thirsty. He was hungry to see the manifested power of the living God *pass to his generation* as Elijah was taken into Heaven. This transition of power is recorded in Second Kings 2, and it foreshadowed the passing of the anointing described in Matthew 28:18-20, when Jesus said:

> *And Jesus came and spake unto them, saying, All power is given unto Me in heaven and in earth. Go ye therefore, and teach all nations, baptizing them in the name of the Father, and of the Son, and of the Holy Ghost: Teaching*

them to observe all things whatsoever I have commanded you: and, lo, I am with you alway, even unto the end of the world. Amen (Matthew 28:18-20 KJV).

For centuries the Church has been standing on that mount, as it were, gazing up into Heaven, expecting Jesus to do from Heaven what He has empowered us to do through the Holy Spirit *on the earth!* The magnitude of God's move in our generation demands that we step down from the mount of spiritual paralysis, take up the mantle of anointing and power Jesus gave us, and begin to *obey His commands.*

HE HAS CALLED US TO FAST, PRAY, AND OBEY

He has called us to fast and pray, and then to obey. At that point, He can release apostolic anointing into our lives, our churches, and our ministry in the world. With this anointing, our ministry will not be apologetic, half-hearted, or apathetic. It will not be laced with fear, doubt, or unbelief. It will be prophetic and apostolic, fitted with a double-edged sharpness that comes only from the Holy Spirit. We will be confrontational without even thinking about it, much as the Lord led me to pray a simple prayer of command through which God literally destroyed the seat of satan in that town in Zaire! The point I am making is that the Spirit of God is driving the Church into the wilderness today! He wants us to learn the lessons of prayer and fasting well so that He can send us out to our generation *in the power of the Spirit!*

If *prayer* is the capsule containing our gifts and requests to God, then *fasting* is the booster rocket that lifts our prayers beyond the boundaries of earth and into the heavenlies. Fasting provides the "oomph" of the Spirit needed to catapult us beyond the gravity of the flesh and into the very purposes of God! When the corporate prayers of the many joined in the name of the One are mounted on the booster rocket of our *corporate fasting*, our prayers suddenly take on a supernatural power that few on earth have ever seen! You can be sure that satan fears this holy combination as no other. Every time God's people have dared to lay aside their differences or personal concerns long enough to seek God in prayer and fasting *together* in one mind and one accord, *terrible things have happened to his dark kingdom*, while wonderful and miraculous things have happened to humankind!

I'm amazed that so few Christians realize that Jesus specifically trained His disciples to fast. He taught them:

Moreover, when you fast, do not be like the hypocrites, with a sad countenance. For they disfigure their faces that they may appear to men to be fasting. Assuredly, I say to you, they have their reward. But you, when you fast, anoint your head and wash your face, so that you do not appear to men to be fasting, but to your Father who is in the secret place; and your Father who sees in secret will reward you openly (Matthew 6:16-18).

Jesus focused on the right motives for fasting, and throughout His discourse, Jesus casually said, "And *when* you fast...." Again notice that Jesus did not say "*if* you decide to," or "*if* you feel so led by the Spirit to one day fast...." No, He spoke of fasting with the same finality and expectation He used when speaking about prayer. He said, "*When* you pray," not "*if*" you pray;

and He said, "*When* you fast," not "if" you fast. Why? Because Jesus *expected* His followers to fast as well as to pray.

THE ABUNDANCE OF RAIN IS COMING!

Fasting moves you from the natural realm into the supernatural realm, and that is the only place you can get supernatural revelation, authorization, and power from the Holy Spirit. As we are in the new millennium, I see the Church in virtually the same place the prophet Elijah was when he prayed for rain on Mount Carmel after he had prophesied to evil King Ahab that rain was coming to end the three-year drought. At first there wasn't a cloud in the sky, but he kept praying.

After a long drought in the Church, we have prophesied that the rains are coming, and like Elijah, we are perched on a high place with our face between our knees. That is the best place we can be! Look again at the story of Elijah:

Then Elijah said to Ahab, "Go up, eat and drink; for there is the sound of abundance of rain." So Ahab went up to eat and drink. And Elijah went up to the top of Carmel; then he bowed down on the ground, and put his face between his knees, and said to his servant, "Go up now, look toward the sea." So he went up and looked, and said, "There is nothing." And seven times he said, "Go again."

Then it came to pass the seventh time, that he said, "There is a cloud, as small as a man's hand, rising out of the sea!" So he said, "Go up, say to Ahab, 'Prepare your chariot, and go down before the rain stops you.'" Now it happened in the meantime that the sky became black with clouds and wind, and there was a heavy rain... (1 Kings 18:41-45).

We are now at the end of our drought in a dry land. The Church is beginning to hear the sound of the abundance of rain! We have seen the first raindrops of God's glory descend in strategic places around the world. A river is starting to rise.

The evidence is clear—as millions have bowed their faces between their knees in earnest intercession and fasting, the Holy Spirit is being poured out afresh on His people. We are witnessing an acceleration of the harvest of souls around the globe. *"There is a cloud, as small as a man's hand, rising out of the sea!"* We boldly prophesy to this generation: *"Prepare yourselves for an outpouring that will lift you from your feet and change the very geography and face of the earth! The river of God is rising to full crest. Prepare to see the earth covered with the glory of God!"*

I believe that we have been doing many things by the might of ourselves in recent years, and we need to take our hands off of this move of God. This is His revival and His harvest. This time, there is no room for the flesh of humanity to glory in His presence or to control and manipulate in His "absence." The sky has become black with clouds and wind, and a *heavy rain* is coming. *This is the **miracle power of God** coming to this generation.*

WE MUST PRAY IT THROUGH!

We are already seeing manifestations of God's glory. As in Ezekiel 47, the river is rising, a new wave of glory that will surpass all others. It will be greater than the Azusa outpouring in the early 1900s. It will outshine the "Latter Rain" and healing revivals in the 1940s and 1950s. It will impact the culture far more than the wave of anointing that swept across America during the Jesus Movement, and it will spark fresh power into the life of the Church that will overshadow the Charismatic outpouring that began in the 1970s. You and I are to be the stewards of this new wave of God's glory, but first we must *pray it through*. Then it will immerse you in God's anointing as never before, take you to places you have never been before, and cause you to do things you have never done before.

By fasting and praying *together*, we can overcome every hindrance, obstruction, and mountain that block the way between us and our corporate destiny and calling in Christ! Victory is only found in the realm of the Spirit, and that is why the devil takes every opportunity to divert us from the mode of prayer and fasting back into the *natural mode*.

I believe God wants the Church to get into the mode of fasting and praying *now* because He knows it will be necessary if we are going to come into the *fullness* of our apostolic mantle, our apostolic ministry, and our apostolic anointing for *miracles and signs and wonders*. The Lord is asking us today, "Will you be a people who will see the vision—My vision—and be willing to *pay the price* through prayer and fasting?" Now let me bring it closer to home: Are *you* willing to pay the price?

Revival and global harvest will never happen unless we become *personally* involved in the purposes of God through obedience in prayer and fasting. The soil of our hearts must be *prepared* to receive the saving seed of Jesus. This can only be done beforehand through the labor of love on our knees before the

Father of all. As we labor on our knees, God releases the *power* that sets people free.

Again, this revival and harvest of souls will not happen the way we think it will, or the way "we've always done it in the past." This move of God will only follow the patterns revealed in God's Word. Paul told the skeptical Corinthians:

> *And my speech and my preaching were not with persuasive words of human wisdom, but in demonstration of the Spirit and of power, that your faith should not be in the wisdom of men but in the power of God* (1 Corinthians 2:4-5).

As we pray and fast, God will give us divine favor with government officials, village leaders, and other "gatekeepers" we may encounter along the way—even the weather.

THAT'S THE POWER OF GOD!

I remember the time Bonnie and I rented a single-engine plane and flew into the interior of Africa to the city of Kikwit in Zaire. The first night there, we preached to 40,000 people, most of whom had never heard the Gospel preached in power. As the power of God fell, a 10-year-old boy who had been totally crippled all his life, instantly began walking! Then, in the power of the Holy Spirit, I said, "There is a giant tumor in someone's stomach, and it is disappearing!" The attorney general of the Bandundu province (which includes Kikwit) was in the crowd that night, and he had been diagnosed with a massive tumor in his intestinal area. He came up and told me in front of the crowd, "It went 'poof!' and went away! I want to serve Jesus all my life!" Now *that's* the power of God.

Not long after our outreach in Kikwit, several mysterious and fatal outbreaks of the deadly Ebola Hemorrhagic Fever occurred in this city. But God had sent His servants to prepare the people of this region with the message of salvation and the power of the Holy Spirit before this deadly outbreak. This reveals the mercy and love of God and is how He wants to use ordinary people like us to confront the enemy and bring the lost to Jesus.

God wants to give us signs and wonders and miracles today for the purpose of furthering the Gospel and glorifying His name. When we answer His command to "Go!" then His signs and wonders will surely follow. But we must be genuinely committed to touch and bless the needy around us as Jesus did. The miracles God gives us are not to be considered "Charismatic playthings" for us to use lightly or giggle about. They are awesome signs of His power and love that must be stewarded humbly for His glory.

I recall the time I held a meeting in the central African bush where thousands of people had gathered. The site was so remote that there were no buildings or tents available to protect the people from the sun or the elements. It was strictly an "open-air" affair. Included among the thousands of people gathered there to hear the Gospel were hundreds of children and little babies.

COMMAND THE CLOUDS TO LEAVE

As I prepared to preach to the people, a tight cluster of dark ominous storm clouds gathered directly over our heads. They weren't scattered evenly over the sky; they were definitely tightly clustered as if they had been moved into position by some unseen force. It would have been disastrous for a downpour to come at that moment. There was simply nowhere to run, and lightning could have made it a potentially fatal situation. I was praying under my breath about the situation when one of the local leaders suddenly announced to the crowd, "And now the man of God from America, Mahesh Chavda, will pray and command the storm clouds to leave!" and he turned to me!

I swallowed hard and stepped forward, thinking, *Lord, I don't know how I got into this spot, but You are the only One who can answer this prayer. Please answer my request in Jesus' name.* Then I asked God to disperse the clouds as the crowd listened (and watched). The clouds broke apart within a few minutes and I was able to continue preaching the Gospel without a single drop of rain falling on the crowd! This miraculous sign and wonder was a great witness of the *power* of God to the Africans, and many came to Jesus that day because of God's open manifestation of His power and might.

The greater the move of God, the greater will be satan's opposition to us at times. As usual, *if we have paid the price in obedience through prayer and fasting*, God has a way of transforming what the enemy meant for evil into something incredibly good. In many cases during the coming harvest, that transformation can literally become a sign and a wonder that itself brings conviction on the unsaved and glory to God.

While ministering in the city of Mbuji-Mayi, a center of sorcery in Kasai, Zaire, thousands of people were born again. The sorcerers and witch doctors had become extremely angry because they were no longer being paid for putting curses on people. The people whom they had cursed were being saved, and *the curses were of no effect*. In other words, the Gospel of Jesus Christ was putting the sorcerers out of business!

Consequently, the sorcerers arranged to send the chief sorcerer to our meeting so he could personally *put a curse on me*. As I was praying for people in several prayer lines, this chief sorcerer pretended he was sick so he could blend in with the hundreds of people waiting for prayer. Unknown to me, he ended up in the third line. The local pastors knew who he was, but they were so afraid of the power of his curses that they kept silent about this man's identity.

The sorcerer was a tall man wearing a necklace of human bones. As I approached him, he started rumbling; then he uttered a noise that was beyond human agency. It sounded like a combination of 14 or 15 different animal voices. My hair stood on end as I heard the growlings and saw his eyes roll back in his head. I had clear discernment of what I was dealing with, and I said to myself, "This man must need a lot of help."

I did not come up with any brilliant prayer for his deliverance. I simply said, "*Jesus, bless him.*"

THE WITCH DOCTOR "STUCK" TO THE GROUND

As I spoke the words, it was as if thousands of volts of electricity hit the chief sorcerer's body. He was flung about 10 feet through the air and violently hit the dirt. Each time he tried to get up, he found that he couldn't move an inch. That made him

The Hidden Power of Prayer and Fasting

roar and growl all the louder! He was glued to the ground as if an angel had been commissioned to sit on him. I said, "Well, Lord, You know what You're doing. Bless him."

Some time later I found this man testifying to the local pastors. He explained that he could not get up from the ground until he confessed Jesus Christ as Lord. When he looked at me, his eyes grew wide, and he shook his finger at me and said, "I know spirits. But the Spirit over this man is greater than any spirit I've ever seen!" This ex-sorcerer was simply seeing the supernatural power of the Holy Spirit at work.

God will also move in new and unusual ways in this great harvest—even from a distance using unorthodox means (after all, He is God, and He can do whatever He wants to do). While conducting evangelistic outreaches in Costa Rica, our services were broadcast live over the radio to several surrounding countries. On the third day, a woman who had listened to the ministry by radio actually came to the meeting and said that she wanted to share her testimony. She told us this amazing story of God's healing power:

"I was listening to this man [pointing to me] on the radio broadcast three days ago. I had a giant tumor the size of a grapefruit growing inside my throat. As I heard this man preaching the Word of God, the tumor started vibrating. While he preached, the tumor shook more and more violently. Suddenly it burst inside my throat lining and came out of my mouth."

When this woman went to her doctors, they took 18 separate x-rays of her throat over the next 36-hour period and were unable to find a single trace of the malignant tumor that had

202

been there before God intervened! It is significant to me that I wasn't there to lay my hands on this woman. The Holy Spirit honored the preaching of God's Word by healing her.

Very often, God will work through us when we "don't feel a thing," just to prove to us that it is God who does the work, not you or me. In this revival, no flesh will be able to steal God's glory by claiming to perform those things only God can perform. I remember another time when I was pastoring in Texas and a family drove hundreds of miles from New Mexico to come to our church for prayer.

NOTHING TO DO WITH FEELINGS

This family had five young children, two of whom were small babies. Their need was especially acute because their mother's body was almost totally consumed with cancer. As I laid hands on that woman, *I did not feel an ounce of anointing.* At that time, I had no faith for her healing, but I said, "O Lord, look on these little ones, and *have mercy* on this family."

The very next day, the family requested tests on the mother at a hospital in the neighboring city. The tests revealed that there wasn't even a trace of cancer left in her body! All the malignancy had disappeared. I was able to touch the heart of God in this case by crying out for the Lord's *mercy* just as Bartimaeus did in the New Testament. God's call has nothing to do with our feelings or with circumstances. As soldiers of the Lord, we are commanded to be "instant in season and out of season" in all things.[2] Again, because of the magnitude of the harvest before us, we need to learn how to minister "in His rest" instead of in our own effort or personal resources.

Another unique characteristic of this revival is the way God will use young people and children to bring in the harvest. I also believe He will use them in ways that may seem totally unusual and odd to us, but it will still be God. I was ministering in Houston one time when I prayed for a group of 70 children who had come forward to be filled with the Holy Spirit. The anointing came upon them and they began to fall under the power of the Spirit, speaking in tongues and weeping.

Among these children was a 5-year-old Mexican boy who began to violently cry out to the Lord in tongues while tears streamed down his face. He was plugged into the power of God for about 20 minutes when suddenly a man burst into loud sobs in the back of the auditorium. A Mexican gentleman came forward and stood with the little boy, who turned out to be the man's son. As this father gave his life to Jesus Christ and was filled with the Spirit, I realized that the little boy *had been praying through* for his daddy.

YOUNG WARRIORS ARE ARISING!

We will literally see the ancient prophecy come to pass in this great harvest: "*Your sons and your daughters will prophesy!*" I am absolutely convinced that God will use a new army of young warriors to carry much of the weight and momentum of this great harvest. There are already deep rumblings in many nations, a vast army of children and teens that is beginning to awaken from their sleep. We may not see them now, but they are coming. Those of us who are older must be ready to accept them, encourage them, and wisely direct them in the things of God.

But above all, we must not hinder or forbid them from answering the call of God!

Finally, this revival and great harvest will recognize no boundaries, barriers, walls, or preferences. If anything, God will go out of His way to touch the poor, the outcast, the forgotten, and the lowly among us! We must have the same heart as our Master or we will be left behind and wish we had yielded.

While ministering in Zaire, Africa, I was put right in the middle of a miraculous visitation of God with crowds of more than 200,000 per night. We were overwhelmed by the sheer number of people who came forward each night for prayer, so we decided to designate one day in which we would do nothing but lay our hands on the critically sick or dying.

I went to the arena expecting to see 1,000 people or so waiting for prayer, but instead I saw a crowd of 25,000 people waiting for me there! I had given my word to lay hands on each one of them, so I took a deep breath and began to pray. Some of the people had literally been brought to the arena in wheelbarrows, and many of the people had a nauseatingly foul odor because they had not been cleansed of their bodily fluids for days.

"I Am Glad to Be Here With You"

In that tropical climate, the foul by-products of sickness become a hundred times worse. There were many lepers in the crowd, along with people with horrible fungus growths on their bodies. Hundreds of people who were dying from the final phase of AIDS came forward for prayer as well. No matter what terrible sickness wracked their bodies, I had one mandate from my

Savior, and it is the same mandate He has given to you. I held them in my arms and told them Jesus loves them, and I prayed the prayer of faith for their healing and for their salvation.

As I did this, I literally felt the pleasure of the Holy Spirit. He said to me, "I am glad to be here with you." Then to *my* delight He healed many of those desperate people!

This is the hour when power is going to be seen in the Church of Jesus Christ as never before. We have received a sovereign commission to set our cities and nations free from the yoke of satan, but all this is dependent on our willingness to be led by the Spirit and to pay the price for the *power* of God.

Just as the requirements of a massive invasion are dramatically different from the requirements of a small skirmish, so are the requirements of *global revival and harvest* different from the needs of small local or isolated evangelistic outreach efforts. God is calling for His "big guns" this time. He is calling for "all hands" in a total Church mobilization. He wants to see the full complement of His "officer corps" brought to the front, and He is prepared to give us powerful signs and wonders to explode the strongholds of the enemy and to remove the obstacles blocking the way to cities and nations. But *first, God's people must fast and pray*—then He will release His apostolic anointing through a flood of His glory and bring in a harvest such as this world has never seen.

Are you ready? Do you want *more* of Him? Then it is time to tap the hidden power of prayer and fasting.

ENDNOTES

1. We videotaped these testimonies by eyewitnesses as they were given to us in the city of Kananga, Zaire.

2. See 2 Timothy 4:2 KJV.

Additional copies of this book and other
book titles from DESTINY IMAGE are
available at your local bookstore.

For a complete list of our titles,
visit us at www.destinyimage.com
Send a request for a catalog to:

Destiny Image® Publishers, Inc.
P.O. Box 310
Shippensburg, PA 17257-0310

*"Speaking to the Purposes of God for this
Generation and for the Generations to Come."*